CULTURE SMART!
EGYPT

Jailan Zayan

·K·U·P·E·R·A·R·D·

First published in Great Britain 2007
by Kuperard, an imprint of Bravo Ltd
59 Hutton Grove, London N12 8DS
Tel: +44 (0) 20 8446 2440 Fax: +44 (0) 20 8446 2441
www.culturesmartguides.com
Inquiries: sales@kuperard.co.uk

Culture Smart! is a registered trademark of Bravo Ltd

Distributed in the United States and Canada
by Random House Distribution Services
1745 Broadway, New York, NY 10019
Tel: +1 (212) 572-2844 Fax: +1 (212) 572-4961
Inquiries: csorders@randomhouse.com

Series Editor Geoffrey Chesler
Design Bobby Birchall

ISBN 978 1 85733 342 8

British Library Cataloguing in Publication Data
A CIP catalogue entry for this book is available from the
British Library

Printed in Malaysia

Cover image: Wall relief at Saqqara. *Travel Ink/Abbie Enock*
Images on pages 13, 17, 60, 91, 102, 105, 106, 123, 125, 141, and 164 by permission
of the Egyptian State Tourist Office, London
The photograph on page 36 is reproduced by permission of the Eardley family.

CultureSmart!Consulting and **Culture Smart!** guides have both
contributed to and featured regularly in the weekly travel program
"Fast Track" on BBC World TV.

About the Author

JAILAN ZAYAN is a British national of Libyan–Egyptian origin. After graduating in law from the School of Oriental and African Studies, University of London, she took up a career in journalism, working for several news organizations. She moved to Egypt in 2000, where she reported and contributed articles to international and Middle Eastern publications about the Arab world, specifically Egypt. She is currently a Cairo-based reporter for Agence France-Presse.

Other Books in the Series

- Culture Smart! Argentina
- Culture Smart! Australia
- Culture Smart! Belgium
- Culture Smart! Botswana
- Culture Smart! Brazil
- Culture Smart! Britain
- Culture Smart! China
- Culture Smart! Costa Rica
- Culture Smart! Cuba
- Culture Smart! Czech Republic
- Culture Smart! Denmark
- Culture Smart! Finland
- Culture Smart! France
- Culture Smart! Germany
- Culture Smart! Greece
- Culture Smart! Hong Kong
- Culture Smart! Hungary
- Culture Smart! India
- Culture Smart! Ireland
- Culture Smart! Israel
- Culture Smart! Italy
- Culture Smart! Japan
- Culture Smart! Korea
- Culture Smart! Mexico
- Culture Smart! Morocco
- Culture Smart! Netherlands
- Culture Smart! New Zealand
- Culture Smart! Norway
- Culture Smart! Panama
- Culture Smart! Peru
- Culture Smart! Philippines
- Culture Smart! Poland
- Culture Smart! Portugal
- Culture Smart! Russia
- Culture Smart! Singapore
- Culture Smart! South Africa
- Culture Smart! Spain
- Culture Smart! Sweden
- Culture Smart! Switzerland
- Culture Smart! Thailand
- Culture Smart! Turkey
- Culture Smart! Ukraine
- Culture Smart! USA
- Culture Smart! Vietnam

Other titles are in preparation. For more information, contact: info@kuperard.co.uk

The publishers would like to thank **CultureSmart!**Consulting for its help in researching and developing the concept for this series.

contents

contents

Map of Egypt

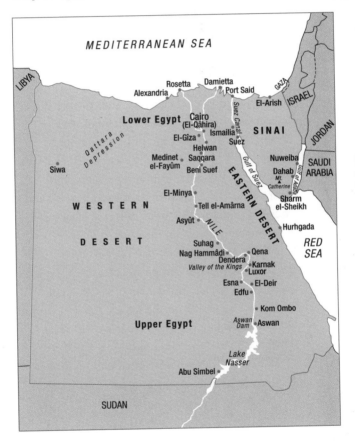

introduction

To many, the idea of Egypt conjures up a picture of the great pyramids and sphinx towering over the empty desert. But these monuments are merely the best known of many treasures left by the remarkable civilization of Ancient Egypt. For thousands of years the fertile banks of the Nile have been home to human settlement, and throughout its history Egypt has exchanged influences with the many different cultures it has encountered. Greeks, Romans, Persians, and Arabs have all left their mark on modern Egyptian society in the form of an astonishing legacy of temples, churches, and mosques.

At first sight, modern-day Egypt is an unruly and chaotic place, a cacophony of sounds, an overload of smells, and a visual theater, all of which can be taxing on the senses. Ancient church domes and medieval minarets share the same space with fast-food chains and Internet cafés.

The country that has inspired conquerors, academics, and artists is home to 79 million people, who call it *Omm Eddunia*, Mother of the World. It is the people who are Egypt's true wealth. They are by nature friendly, cheerful, warm and hospitable, renowned for their sense of humor, and also extremely stubborn and proud.

Good personal relations are at the core of the Egyptian value system. People are more important than time or money.

As in many developing countries, only certain aspects of this traditional and deeply conservative society have been affected by modernization. One can pay telephone bills on the Internet, though more than half the population is illiterate. Televisions in fashionable cafés play daring music videos, with the call to prayer booming from loudspeakers five times a day. In Egypt each individual finds his or her way of coping with change while trying to uphold traditional values.

This book explores the codes and paradoxes of Egyptian life. It outlines the country's history and shows the forces that have shaped its sensibility. It explains values and attitudes, and guides you through local customs and traditions. It opens a window into the private lives of Egyptians, how they behave at home, and how they interact with foreign visitors. It offers practical advice, from how to make friends to avoiding *faux pas.*

Culture Smart! Egypt sets out to make that first trip as rich as possible, to take you beyond the clichés to the real people. Welcome to Egypt, *Ahlan wa Sahlan*!

Key Facts

Official Name	Arab Republic of Egypt	Egypt is a member of the Arab League and the African Union.
Capital City	Cairo	Population approx. 15 million
Main Cities	Alexandria, Port Said, Suez, Asyût	
Population	78.9 million (July 2006 estimate)	Population growth rate 1.75% (2006 est.)
Ethnic Makeup	Egyptian 98%; Berber, Bedouin and Beja 1%; Greek, Armenian, and other European 1%	
Age Structure	0-14 years: 32.6% 15-64 years: 62.9% 65 years and over: 4.5%	
Area	387,000 sq. miles (1,001,000 sq. km)	
Geography	Situated at northeast corner of Africa. Bordered by Libya, Sudan, Israel, and Gaza	Four regions: Delta and Nile Valley, Western Desert, Eastern Desert, Sinai Peninsula
Terrain	Desert plateau interrupted by Nile valley and delta	The Nile flows through the country, dividing at Cairo to form the Delta.
Climate	Hot, dry summers and mild winters	
Natural Resources	Petroleum, natural gas, iron ore, phosphates, manganese, limestone, gypsum, talc, asbestos, lead, zinc	

Currency	Egyptian pound (LE or EP)	
Language	Arabic	English and French widely understood by educated classes
Religion	Mostly Sunni Muslim; approx.10% Coptic Christian	
Minority Faiths	Shi'a Muslim, Greek Orthodox and other Christians, Baha'i, Jewish	
Government	Egypt is a republic. Bicameral legislature. President is head of state, elected by popular vote for six-year term	
Media	Some television channels and newspapers are state owned. There are a number of privately owned satellite TV channels.	The three main government papers are *Al Ahram*, *Al Akhbar*, and *Al Gomhouria*. The liberal *Al Masry el Youm* is independent.
Electricity	220 volts (50 Hz)	2-pronged plugs used
DVD/Video	TV/video is PAL system; DVD is European region	
Telephone	Egypt's country code is 20.	To dial out of Egypt, dial 00 and then the country code.
Time Zone	GMT +2 hours During the summer, it is GMT +3 hours.	

chapter one

LAND &
PEOPLE

GEOGRAPHY

Egypt enjoys a special location at the northeastern corner of the African continent. Standing at the crossroads of Africa, Europe, and Asia, it has always been a focal point for trade routes between the continents. It is bordered by Libya to the west, the Mediterranean Sea to the north, the Gaza Strip and Israel to the east, the Red Sea on the east coast, and Sudan to the south. The Suez Canal, which runs from the Mediterranean city of Port Said to Suez City on the Red Sea, cuts through the stretch of land that connects mainland Egypt to the Sinai Peninsula. It spans a total area of 387,000 square miles (1,001,000 sq. km).

Egypt's pumping heart is the River Nile, which supplies the country with all its water. Rising from sources in Ethiopia and Uganda, it snakes northward through Sudan to the Mediterranean coast. As it passes Cairo, it splits into two, forming the Delta. Egypt's most fertile stretch of land, this is host to a network of canals and channels around which villages have formed.

Away from the Delta and the Nile Valley, the terrain is mostly desert. In an effort to increase the cultivable area, the government has reclaimed the desert in different parts of the country and encouraged the settlement of new communities.

Egypt can be divided into four regions: the Delta and Nile Valley, the Western Desert, the Eastern Desert, and the Sinai Peninsula.

The fan-shaped Delta covers an area of about 14,000 square miles (22,000 sq. km). The Nile Valley from Cairo to Aswan is a 621-mile (1,000-km) long, narrow stretch of cultivated land. Lake Nasser, between Aswan and Abu Simbel in the south, is the world's largest artificial lake (formed by the huge Aswan Dam), covering an astounding 2,027 square miles (5,250 sq. km) area.

The Eastern Desert, which occupies almost a quarter of Egypt's land surface, is a barren plateau, indented occasionally by cliffs and mountains on its eastern edge. The Western Desert, the largest in Egypt (259,000 sq. miles, 671,000 sq. km), stretches from the Nile Valley into Libya, and is rich in natural resources, including gold, coal, and oil. Its unforgiving aridity is broken by a series of green oases, the largest of which is Siwa, near the Libyan border.

The Sinai Peninsula is a triangular wedge to the east of the Suez Canal. Its southern part is mountainous and includes Gabal Catreen, or Mount Catherine, the country's highest point, towering over the desert at 8,667 feet (2,642 m) high. Heading north, the topography becomes flatter as it reaches the Mediterranean coast.

CLIMATE

Egypt has two main seasons: a hot summer and a mild winter. Winter, from November to March, is cool, with occasional rainfall. Summer, from May to September, is fierce. Average temperatures range from 57°F (14°C) in winter and 86°F (30°C) in summer. Inland temperatures can reach 44°F (7°C) in winter and 109°F (43°C) in summer.

Hot dust storms, the Khamasin, occur after winter. The term comes from the Arabic word *khamsin*, which means "fifty," because the winds are said to occur at any time in a fifty-day period between March and June. Humidity is high near the coasts, and highest along the north coast.

PEOPLE

Egypt is the second-most populous country in Africa, with 79 million inhabitants, most of whom are settled around the Nile, and half of whom live in urban areas. It has one of the highest population densities in the world and, with the rapid growth in population, towns and cities have had to spread, eating up valuable agricultural land.

People in rural areas are mainly involved in agriculture; villages have formed around water sources, canals, and irrigation channels. An agrarian peasant is called a *fellah* (plural, *fellahin*). Upper Egyptians, who live south of Cairo around the Nile Valley, are referred to as Si'idi. Egypt's desert dwellers are Bedouin, originally descended from Arab and Berber tribes. Nubian communities live in the south.

A BRIEF HISTORY

Egypt has a spectacularly rich cultural history, influenced by contact over millennia with many very different societies and civilizations. Yet, from ancient times to the present, Egyptian society has remained predominantly agricultural, and the Nile has remained the bountiful provider in an otherwise barren desert. These factors have helped to maintain a link between the Egyptians of antiquity with their modern descendants, and find an echo in persisting traditions and attitudes.

During its history, Egypt has often risen to greatness, dominating its neighbors culturally and politically; at other times it has been overshadowed by, if not subservient to, them. Yet, until recently, the productiveness of the land has meant that even the times of adversity have not lasted—given the right conditions, Egypt repeatedly reassumed a leading cultural and political role. This frequent exchange of roles, from dominant empire to exploited dependency, is another important feature of Egyptian history that affects the Egyptians of today, who take it as given that it is only a matter of time before Egypt resumes its leading role among the nations.

Ancient Egypt (6000 BCE –323 BCE)

Archaeological evidence shows that primitive farming along the banks of the Nile began at least as early as the tenth millennium BCE. In around 8000 BCE climatic changes desiccated large areas of North Africa, forcing groups of pastoralists to converge on the Nile Valley and stimulating the development of advanced agricultural communities. To this day Egyptians live along the Nile, separated from other population centers to the west and east by hundreds of miles of desert.

Around 6000 BCE the Egyptians were growing cereal crops and herding animals, constructing large buildings, and using metal tools. By the fourth millennium BCE they were trading with neighboring lands and had developed proto-hieroglyphics. By the end of this millennium there

existed two separate states in the land of Egypt—
northern (Lower) Egypt and southern (Upper)
Egypt. Around 3100 BCE the ruler of Upper Egypt
conquered Lower Egypt and united all of Egypt
for the first time. This was the Pharaoh Narmer
(or Menes). He and his successors established a
ruling house that is referred to as the First
Dynasty of Ancient Egypt.

Pharaonic history is traditionally divided into
thirty-one dynasties. Narmer's First Dynasty
initiated Ancient Egyptian history, while the

Thirty-First brought it to a
close in 332 BCE, the date of
Alexander the Great's arrival
in Egypt. Groups of dynasties
have been combined by
historians to define three
"Kingdoms": Old (Third to
Sixth Dynasties), Middle (Eleventh to
Thirteenth), and New (Eighteenth to Twentieth),
as well as a Late Period (Twenty-Fifth to Thirty-
First). Each of the three "Kingdoms" lasted for
about four to five centuries. The pharaohs who
ruled during these periods and the monuments
they erected are those most familiar to us today.

The dynasties outside these three "Kingdoms"
mostly ruled at times of civil war and disunity or
partial or total foreign domination. Particularly
after the end of the New Kingdom, several

dynasties were foreign, and weak Egyptian rulers yielded control of Egypt to Libyan, Nubian, Assyrian, and Persian dynasties.

Greco-Roman Egypt (332 BCE–330 CE)
Egypt became part of the huge empire of Alexander the Great in 332 BCE, and thus began almost a millennium of Greek influence. On his death in 323, Alexander's empire, which extended from Greece to northern India, started to crumble. Egypt became the independent realm of the Macedonian general Ptolemy, a close companion of

Alexander. He declared himself king in 305, thus founding the Ptolemaic dynasty and making Egypt an imperial center once more.

Ptolemaic Egypt (323–30 BCE)
Though Alexander spent little time in Egypt before his death, he laid the foundations for the city of Alexandria. The Ptolemies made Alexandria their new capital, and for centuries it was the greatest city of antiquity. Its famous lighthouse on the island of Pharos was one of the Seven Wonders of the World, while its magnificent library was the world's first state-funded scientific institution and attracted scholars from around the Hellenized world.

The Ptolemaic rulers adopted Egyptian customs and dress, built temples for Egyptian gods, and took on the role of the ancient pharaohs. Nevertheless, as thousands of Greeks migrated to Egypt, a dual culture was established. The rulers and the Greek immigrants, who enjoyed special privileges, together with the wealthier Egyptian classes, forged a Greco-Egyptian, Greek-speaking society. Meanwhile, the bulk of the farming population, especially in Upper Egypt, were left largely undisturbed. The pattern of a privileged foreign ruling class with an alien culture—remaining separate from the mass of the mainly peasant population with its local language and customs—is one that was to repeat itself over the course of history as various overseas powers exchanged control of Egypt.

For much of the fourth and third centuries BCE, Ptolemaic Egypt was one of the most powerful states in the Eastern Mediterranean. Yet, by the second century BCE, it was weakened by internal instability as members of the dynasty fought each other for supremacy. By this time Rome was the dominant power in the Mediterranean.

The last Ptolemaic ruler, the famous Cleopatra VII, became involved in Roman politics, first as the lover of Julius Caesar, and then, after Caesar's assassination, as the ally and lover of Mark Anthony in the continuing Roman

civil war. They were defeated by the forces of Octavian, who became the first Roman emperor, Augustus. Cleopatra committed suicide and her son by Caesar was killed, thus ending Ptolemaic rule.

Roman Egypt (30 BCE–330 CE)

Like the Ptolemies, Roman emperors appear in the traditional pharaonic form on the walls of Egyptian temples. However, Egypt was now an imperial province and no longer the center of an empire, though it prospered economically under Roman rule, at least until the third century CE. Rome's primary interest in Egypt was its supply of grain, but it also became an important base for Roman trade with the East.

There was no large Roman population in Egypt and Latin was never adopted by the Egyptians. The Greek-speaking elite continued to dominate cultural life, while local culture remained alive in the countryside. Egyptian religious customs continued, and Egyptian temples remained in use.

Alexandria was surpassed in greatness by Rome, but kept its position as the second city of the Mediterranean world. It remained the principal center of Hellenistic learning.

Christianity

The history of early Christianity has many links with Egypt. The Holy Family is believed to have

sought sanctuary in Egypt during the infancy of
Jesus. The first Egyptian Christians are believed to
have been converted by Mark the Evangelist, who
therefore is considered the first Egyptian patriarch
(or pope). Alexandria hosted the very first
Christian catechetical school. Celebrated Doctors
of the Church, notably Origen, St. Athanasius,
and St. Cyril of Alexandria, were Egyptians. It was
in Egypt that both the Arian and Nestorian
heresies were born. Many even
believe the Christian symbol of the
Cross first came into use in Egypt
and that it was partially derived
from the Egyptian Ankh cross—the
symbol of life.

Perhaps the most important contribution of
Egypt to Christianity was monasticism. This
developed in the third century, when many
Egyptian Christians, threatened by persecution,
fled to the desert to set up new communities far
from the reach of the state. In the fourth century
Egyptians such as St. Anthony and Pachomius
developed monastic rules and ideas, which spread
to the rest of the Christian world.

Byzantine Rule (330–642)
Although Egyptian Christianity started in
Alexandria, most converts were Egyptian and not
Greek, and by about 200 CE Christianity had

spread throughout Egypt's towns and into rural areas. The Scriptures were translated into the Greek-influenced Egyptian language used at the time, known today as Coptic, which remains the official language of the Egyptian Coptic Church.

Christians were persecuted by the Romans until the end of the third century, but in the early fourth century Christianity became the official religion of the Byzantine Empire (as the later Roman Empire is called). The numbers of Christians increased greatly, as did hostility toward pagan forms of worship. In 391, the Emperor Theodosius ordered all heathen temples to be destroyed, and paganism was outlawed throughout the Empire. Among the buildings demolished was the Library of Alexandria, a bastion of classical learning. Attacks on pagan temples by fanatical monks are recorded as late as the fifth century and it is likely that no pagans survived into the seventh century. Christianity thus extinguished the ancient religions, the roots of which went back to pharaonic Egypt. But Egyptian religious identity remained independent, and expressed itself through the new faith.

The Coptic Church

In the two centuries that followed the adoption of Christianity by the Empire, the leading clergy, including Egyptian bishops, conducted doctrinal debates about the "nature" of Christ. These sometimes resulted in schisms and shaped the history of the Church.

Political maneuvering between the dioceses of Alexandria and Rome contributed to the outcome of the Council of Chalcedon in 451. This council repudiated the Monophysite doctrine associated with the Alexandrian Church—that in Christ there was but one nature—and removed the Alexandrian patriarch from office.

Most Egyptian clergymen rejected this, as did the bulk of the population, and reacted by appointing their own patriarch. A new Egyptian Church was born, independent of the bishops of Rome and Constantinople: the Coptic Church. For almost two centuries Copts came under pressure from the Byzantine state to renounce their "heresy." Torture and execution were sometimes used, causing great resentment of Byzantine rule among the Egyptians and focusing their national identity on the Coptic Church.

Islamic Egypt

At the beginning of the seventh century a new religion was born in western Arabia that was to change the world. By 634 the tribes of Arabia had united under the banner of this new religion, Islam. Muslim Arab armies defeated the forces of the two main powers of the region: Sassanid Persia and the Byzantine Empire.

After ten years of fighting, most
of the Middle East had fallen to
the Muslim troops. Within another
decade the Sassanid Empire was no
more, and the Byzantines were confined
to their territories in the Balkans, Greece, and Asia
Minor. An Islamic empire had been created that,
at its territorial peak in the early eighth century,
stretched from the Atlantic to the Indian Ocean.

Province of the Caliphate (642–868)

After defeats in Syria in the mid-630s, the
Byzantines were on the defensive. By 642, Egypt
was fully occupied by the Muslims. Egypt now
became a province of the Caliphate, as the
Muslim empire was known. The mostly Coptic
Egyptian population did not lament the departure
of the Byzantines. Local communities were well
treated by the Muslims: Islamic law stated that
"People of the Book," that is, Jews and Christians,
who lived under Muslim rule were protected and
not to be harmed. Muslims rarely pressured local
populations to convert, and in Egypt conversion
to Islam was a slow process. It is estimated it took
about seven centuries for the Muslim population
of Egypt to exceed the 50 percent mark.

As Alexandria was subject to Byzantine raids
and was even briefly reoccupied in the 640s, the
Muslims built a new capital inland, just east of the

apex of the Delta. The new town, called al-Fustat, was also more accessible to reinforcements from Syria in case of need.

Egypt spent two centuries as a Muslim province supplying the reigning caliphs with revenue from agricultural taxation. Arab tribes settled along the Nile Valley. While these were too few in number to affect the country's ethnic or religious composition, they were important in disseminating the Arabic language.

Egyptian Muslim Empires

The caliphs were the political successors of the Prophet Mohammed. The first caliphs originally ruled from Medina in western Arabia. They were followed in 661 by the Umayyad caliphs, who ruled from Damascus. In 750 the Abbasids took over, and established their capital in Baghdad.

During its first two centuries, Islam had divided into two main branches, Sunnism and Shi'ism. Shi'ism further split into different groups: the main group, Imami, tended to be distanced from political activism; another group, the Isma'ili Shi'is, became militantly anti-Abbasid, especially in the ninth century. The caliphs and main political forces were Sunni and easily kept the Shi'is and other political opponents in check. In the ninth century, however, the Caliphate began to weaken, and the peripheries became detached.

As the Abbasid Caliphate weakened, Egypt began to gravitate toward political independence. Ibn Tulun, the Abbasid general sent to govern Egypt in 868, was independent of Baghdad in all but name. His armies kept the Caliphate's forces at bay, and he expanded Egyptian control into Palestine and Syria. The pattern was repeated by al-Ikhshid, who controlled Egypt from 935.

In the early tenth century a rebellion of Isma'ili Shi'is erupted in many provinces of the Caliphate, where they managed to create scattered independent states. Egypt came under threat from one of these, based in Mahdiya, in modern-day Tunisia, created by a dynasty called the Fatimids. They extended their control over most of North Africa and even proclaimed themselves caliphs in opposition to the Sunni Caliph in Baghdad.

The Fatimid Caliphate (969–1157)

The Fatimids invaded Egypt in 969, and by 970 their armies had reached Syria, aiming to topple the Abbasid Caliphate in Baghdad. The Fatimid rulers decided to move their capital to Egypt, which was closer to their enemies in Iraq, and extremely wealthy. They built a new city just north of the old Muslim center of al-Fustat. The new capital was called al-Qahira (The Victorious), and has become known in English as Cairo.

Despite early successes against the Abbasids,

the Fatimids never managed to conquer Iraq, and spent a century fighting in northern Syria against the Abbasids and the Byzantines.

In the eleventh century, Turkish tribes from Central Asia broke through the Caliphate's weak eastern defenses. The Turks, newly converted to Islam, established the powerful Seljuk sultanate (kingdom) in the territories of the Abbasid Caliph, who became a political figurehead in their hands. They attacked the Fatimids in Syria.

Meanwhile, the Fatimids had created a powerful regional empire centered on Egypt, which included much of North Africa, Syria, and western Arabia, and trading colonies in Yemen and western India. The early rulers opened up trade routes to India, and Egypt prospered. Cairo started to rival Baghdad in its splendor and prosperity: commerce and industry flourished and it became an intellectual and artistic center.

Soon, however, the Fatimid state was embroiled in power struggles. It was no match for the armies of the First Crusade, which conquered Syria and Palestine in 1098–9. The Crusaders repeatedly rebuffed the Fatimid attempts to retake Palestine.

In the twelfth century, a small but powerful new Turkish state established itself in inland Syria. Realizing the importance of Egypt,

the Crusaders and the Syrian Turks vied to bring
Egypt under their control. The Turks eventually
triumphed and thus the tottering Fatimid
Caliphate fell. The general commanding the
Turkish forces in Egypt was a Kurd by the name of
Salah al-Din, known in the West as Saladin.

The Ayyubids (1157–1250)
Empowered by the wealth of Egypt, Saladin
united Egypt and inland Syria before
turning to deal with the Crusaders on
the coast. In 1157, he destroyed their
armies at Hattin near the Sea of Galilee,
after which he captured Jerusalem.
The Crusaders were left clinging on
to isolated coastal cities. The Third
Crusade bought them a reprieve, but
they were never again a power in the region.

Saladin and his family established the Ayyubid
sultanate, which continued to rule Egypt and
Syria. He built the massive Cairo Citadel, which
became Cairo's military headquarters and
remained so until the twentieth century.

The pattern of power in the Ayyubid dynasty
followed the Turkish model, which relied on a
loose alliance between the leading members of the
ruling family and local tribal chiefs—in the
Ayyubid case, Kurdish as well as Turkish minor
leaders in Syria. This meant that the ruler lacked

absolute power, had to rely on consensus, and had continuously to keep his many allies pleased. The result was an unstable political system. The Europeans began to send fresh Crusades, most of which were now aimed at Egypt—they had come to the conclusion that to control the Holy Land they had to control prosperous and populous Egypt. Eventually, the internal instability of the Ayyubids and repeated Crusader attacks led the army to rebel against the Ayyubid sultan and, in 1250, to take power.

The Mamluks (1250–1517)

The last but one Ayyubid ruler had decided to build a new army loyal to himself alone: an army of slaves, mainly of Turkish origin. Slave soldiers, called Mamluks (literally "owned," in Arabic), were not a new idea and had been used before. They had no legal method of ruling directly, and in the past, when powerful, had at most managed to manipulate princes or caliphs, and united only along narrow factional lines. The Ayyubid Mamluks now faced the same problem and vied with each other for power.

Events were unfolding that would force them to unite. Pagan Mongols had broken through in the East and proceeded to lay waste the cities of Iran. In 1258 they reached Baghdad, which they destroyed, and executed the Abbasid Caliph. In 1259 they advanced into Syria. The Mamluk generals came together and set out to meet them. At Ain Jalut in Palestine the Mongols suffered their first-ever defeat in a pitched battle. The Mongol tide had reached its limit, and the Mamluk sultans finally won legitimacy as the saviors of Islam.

The Mamluks almost immediately set about

ridding the Levant of the other lingering enemy, the Crusaders. By 1291, Acre, in Palestine, the last major city held by the Crusaders, was captured. Egypt and Syria were united once more under the Mamluk sultans, ruling from Cairo.

The Mamluk state now became the center of Arab-Muslim culture. Iraq and eastward had fallen to the Mongols; Mongol rulers over successor states there had converted to Islam but had adopted Persian or Turkish as their official language. With Baghdad destroyed, Cairo was now the first city of Islam, and in the fourteenth century was the largest city in the world.

Egypt became a hub for trade between East and West. Since the Crusades, European demand for Eastern products, especially spices, had increased dramatically and the volume of this trade was huge and profitable. Egypt's prosperity is reflected in the architectural heritage of Mamluk Cairo.

In the fourteenth century, however, plague ravaged Egypt and Syria. A series of insufficient floods in Egypt, and a devastating invasion of Mamluk-controlled Syria by the Turco-Mongol warlord Tamerlane in 1400, led to long periods of famine and starvation in both countries. By the fifteenth century the Mamluk state was in economic distress and resorted to increasing taxation on international trade. One of the effects of soaring prices of imported goods in Europe was that Europeans began to invest in exploring alternative routes to the East.

Rise of the Ottomans

By this time a new power had risen in the north— the Ottoman sultanate. In 1453 the Ottoman Turks had captured Constantinople and finally destroyed the ancient Byzantine Empire. Their armies controlled southeastern Europe, and began to strengthen their positions along the northern borders of Mamluk Syria.

In 1516, Ottoman forces entered Syria. The Mamluks attempted to defend it, but their troops lacked training, their generals were incompetent, and, most importantly, they had failed to appreciate the latest advance in military technology—guns. They continued to believe that victory in battle depended on massed heavy cavalry charges. The professional Ottoman army, which included musket regiments and field artillery, devastated the Mamluk cavalry. In 1517 the Ottoman army marched into Cairo, and hanged the last Mamluk sultan from its gates.

Ottoman Province (1517–1805)

For the next three centuries Egypt once more assumed the role of an imperial dominion, even if a prosperous one. Excess revenues were exported to the Ottoman capital of Istanbul (previously

Constantinople), and skilled workers and artisans moved to the new imperial capital. For the first time since the seventh century, the official language of the empire to which Egypt belonged was no longer Arabic. Higher intellectual activity was carried out in Istanbul in Turkish.

By the eighteenth century, the Ottoman Empire had lost its place as a world power to the new European nation-states. Egypt's governors began to push for more autonomy. However, in 1798, Europe, for long nibbling at the edges of the Ottoman Empire, attempted to conquer some of its central lands.

The French Expedition to Egypt (1798–1801)

The French expedition to Egypt—seen as a halfway house to India—was part of Napoleon's campaign to defeat the British. The French occupied Egypt quickly, but the invasion of Syria a year later met with failure. In 1801 combined Ottoman and British forces eventually forced them to withdraw their troops. Despite the brevity of the French occupation, the event was to have significant repercussions. It opened the door for more European ventures into Ottoman territory, and it awakened the subjects of the Ottoman Empire, especially Egypt, to its lack of defenses against these advanced foreigners.

Egypt reverted to Ottoman control, but a power struggle began, with the population joining in. In 1805 Muhammad Ali, an Albanian officer of the Ottoman force stationed in Egypt, imposed himself, with the support of Egyptian religious and community leaders, as governor of Egypt.

The Dynasty of Muhammad Ali

With the rise to power of Muhammad Ali (1805–52), Egypt entered its "modern period." Nominally an Ottoman governor, Muhammad Ali proceeded to turn Egypt once more into an imperial center. He made himself absolute ruler, removing political opponents and local threats, which included the very local leaders who had helped bring him to power. He conscripted the Egyptian peasants into a new, modern army, and embarked on an ambitious project of

 industrialization based on the European model. Officers, engineers, doctors, and technicians were trained in Europe, or locally by Europeans. Territorial ambitions led to expansion deep into Sudan, Syria, and western Arabia.

By the 1820s Egypt was a formidable regional power. During conflict with the Ottoman sultan in the 1830s, Egyptian forces twice brought the Ottoman Empire to its knees, and were only prevented from marching into Istanbul by European intervention. Finally, in 1841, Britain and other European powers forced Muhammad Ali to reduce the size of his armed forces and to withdraw permanently from Syria and Arabia. In exchange, the Ottomans granted his descendants hereditary "governorship" of Egypt and Sudan.

Under his successors, especially Isma'il Pasha (1863–79), Egypt reembarked on modernization, particularly in the areas of education, agriculture, and communications. In 1854 Egypt built Africa's first railway line. Most spectacular was the excavation of the Suez Canal, which took eleven years to construct and opened in 1869, greatly increasing Egypt's strategic importance. The cost, however, was astronomically higher than estimated, not least in human life.

Isma'il undertook many large-scale projects, but his financial management was incompetent. Borrowing from European creditors at exorbitant rates eventually led to financial crisis. As usual, the peasants were the first to suffer, as taxes were raised even higher and harsher tax-collection methods were implemented. Egypt was forced to sell its shares in the Suez Canal to Britain at a very low price only six years after the opening. Despite these measures Egypt was declared bankrupt. In 1876 the major creditors, Britain and France, took over financial, and effectively political, control of the country.

Isma'il Pasha was forced to abdicate, and his more pliable son, Tewfik (1879–92), replaced him. The situation was becoming intolerable for many Egyptians. In 1881, an Egyptian army officer named Ahmad Urabi led a successful uprising that forced Tewfik to concede to reforms along nationalist lines. Threatened by this movement, the British landed troops in Alexandria in 1882 and suppressed the national revolt. Egyptian independence was lost once more.

British Occupation

Although nominally an autonomous province of the Ottoman Empire, *de facto* Egypt was ruled by

Britain from 1882. With the outbreak of the First World War in 1914, Egypt was declared independent of the Ottomans and a "British Protectorate," thus formalizing the British presence. The Protectorate ended in 1922 and Egypt was

proclaimed a parliamentary monarchy. Despite gaining formal independence, Egypt was strategically important to the British Empire and Britain remained in control politically and militarily until after the Second World War.

During this period, much of the population stood behind the Wafd Party, which had come into being in 1919 calling for complete British withdrawal from the country. For thirty years, politics in Egypt were tri-polar: the king, who wanted more independence from the British, yet a tame parliament; the Wafd, representing the bulk of the people, critical of both the king and the British; and the British, who used political and military pressure to contain any serious threats to their continued presence in Egypt.

The period gave birth to movements that persist until today, whether Islamic, Egyptian Nationalist or, a little later, Arab Nationalist. Among these movements was the Islamist Muslim Brotherhood, established in 1927, as well as a revolutionary organization within the army known as the Free Officers, in the late 1940s.

Gamal Abd al-Nasser (1952–70)

Growing resentment at the continued British presence after the Second World War, defeat at the hands of the new Israeli state in 1948, and the political and moral corruption of the Egyptian monarch, Farouk I (1936–52), led to a military coup by the Free Officers movement. The driving force was Nasser, a colonel in the Egyptian army.

In 1953, the monarchy was abolished and the Free Officers elected General Mohammed Naguib as president. Yet Naguib proved unwilling to enforce the sweeping political changes that the Free Officers wanted, such as abolishing the parliamentary system. He was removed from power in 1954, and Nasser succeeded him as Egypt's second president.

Apart from Naguib, Nasser was the first ethnic Egyptian to rule Egypt since pharaonic times, and it was a matter of national pride to him that Egypt regain its lost grandeur. The first step was to remove the remaining British presence in the country, and he negotiated a treaty in 1954 according to which the last British troops would leave the Suez Canal area in 1956.

Secondly, he envisaged an ambitious project of industrialization and modernization that would transform Egypt. A dam on the Nile at Aswan would generate power for new factories and protect Egyptian agriculture from the occasionally destructive Nile floods. This, however, would require finance. Nasser first approached the British and the Americans, but was refused, so he turned to the Soviet bloc. The Soviets, in search of new allies in the region, gladly offered to help, with both finance and industrial expertise.

While ideologically the Free Officers were not strictly socialist, Nasser's new regime became so. Property laws were passed that confiscated huge tracts of land from the gigantic estates of the land-owning class created by the dynasty of Muhammad Ali, and redistributed them to the peasants. The economy was closed off, and salaries and property rents were frozen. As a result most of the very large foreign community that ran Egypt's private enterprises decided to leave.

Suez

In 1956, Nasser nationalized the Suez Canal Company, which owned and controlled the canal. Incensed by this move, the British and French governments, who were the majority shareholders, decided to invade. They colluded in the Israeli invasion of Sinai, and used the ensuing war as a pretext to occupy the canal zone. But the

U.S.A. and the Soviet Union opposed this operation and put political pressure on Britain and France, forcing them and the Israelis to withdraw. The outcome was an immense political victory for Nasser and severe defeat for the prestige and power of the old colonial powers.

The victory of 1956 emboldened Nasser, who became a bitter enemy of Western imperialism and supported many African countries in their struggles for independence. Together with leaders such as Jawarhalal Nehru of India and President Tito of Yugoslavia, he formed the Non-aligned Movement, aimed at creating an independent bloc, neither Soviet nor Western, to express the interests of the Third World.

Nasser also became the main champion of the Arab Nationalist cause, which called for a Pan-Arab state that united the Arabic-speaking peoples. A product of this Pan-Arab vision was the short-lived union between Egypt and Syria, the United Arab Republic (UAR), from 1959 to 1961.

The newly created state of Israel was the main obstacle to Arab Nationalism, as it was founded on the land of the Palestinian Arabs, over 700,000 of whom had become refugees as a result.

This combination of positions bolstered Nasser's international image as a hero of the developing world, but it made him enemies in the West. The U.S.A., fearing the threat to its regional interests, increased its support of Israel and looked for an opportunity to curb his power. This would eventually lead to disaster for Egypt, and for the Palestinians whose cause he championed.

The '67 War

Disaster struck in 1967. Israel, supported by the Western powers, launched an all-out offensive against the Egyptians, Jordanians, and Syrians. Taken totally by surprise, the Arab air forces were virtually wiped out on the ground, and Israel then easily occupied the remaining Palestinian land (the West Bank and Gaza), as well as taking Sinai from Egypt and the Golan Heights from Syria.

This was not only a military defeat—it was a crippling blow to both the Egyptian economy and Egypt's political prestige. The Suez Canal became the front line and was closed to shipping. Nasser died three years later and it was left to his successor to try to sort out the mess.

Nasser has been criticized for being a dictator, for his socialist economic policies, and most of all for the disastrous defeat of 1967. Nevertheless, achievements such as nationalizing the Suez Canal, construction of the Aswan Dam, land reforms that benefited most of the destitute Egyptian peasantry, and massive industrial expansion ensured that an estimated four to five million mourners (out of a national population of

some thirty million) attended his funeral
procession, one of the largest in history.

Anwar al-Sadat (1970–81)

The vice president, Sadat, assumed power as
president after Nasser's death in 1970. He
attempted to reach a settlement with the
Israelis that would ensure the return of
Egyptian territories lost in the 1967 War.
In response to the UN's Jarring
Mission report, which proposed a
return to the pre-1967 borders in
exchange for peace, he declared that, if
Israel agreed to withdraw from Sinai and the
Gaza Strip and to implement other provisions
stipulated in the report, Egypt would then "be
ready to enter into a peace agreement with Israel."
When Israel replied that it would not withdraw to
the pre-1967 lines, Sadat prepared for war.

In October 1973 the Egyptians and their Syrian
allies launched a coordinated offensive against the
Israelis. Unready for this, the Israelis suffered
heavy casualties and faced defeat. But they
managed to regain the initiative on both fronts,
defeating the Syrians in the north and encircling
half the Egyptian forces in Sinai.

Politically, however, Sadat had achieved his
objective and brought the Israelis to the
negotiating table. His symbolic visit to Israel in

1977 resulted in a peace treaty in 1979 between
Egypt and Israel, and the return of the Sinai
Peninsula. Other Arab states regarded this as a
betrayal of their joint cause and Egypt was
ostracized; many Egyptians shared this feeling.

Economically, Sadat began to reverse Nasser's
socialist policies, implementing an "Open Door
Policy" that lifted constraints on imports and
foreign investment. These policies benefited many
in the middle classes, and a new business class
began to appear. But government corruption
became more widespread and prices of basic
commodities began to soar, affecting the poor
majority. An attempt to remove bread subsidies in
1977 resulted in riots on an unprecedented scale.
Economic hardship and a clampdown on the
active socialist movement boosted the cause of
Islamic radicals, whose numbers began to swell.
In 1981, Sadat was assassinated by radical
Islamists as he attended an annual military parade
celebrating the campaigns of the 1973 War.

Sadat is remembered in various ways by
Egyptians. Many have a very high opinion of him.
The 1973 War is regarded by most Egyptians as an
all-out victory over Israel that avenged Egypt's
1967 defeat. Peace with Israel ended a costly state
of war and brought the return of Sinai. The
liberalization of the economy brought benefits to
many. For others, Nasser's defiant foreign policies

and, economically, his socialism were correct and were betrayed by Sadat. It is still common to hear Sadatists and Nasserists arguing loudly in both working-class cafés and middle-class homes.

Hosni Mubarak (1981–present)

Following the assassination of Sadat, his vice president, Mubarak, assumed power. Mubarak managed to patch up relations with the rest of the Arab world, at the same time keeping the peace treaty with Israel intact. Unlike his predecessors, he has refrained from taking major political risks, and Egypt has managed to avoid warfare in a politically problematic region.

Internally, however, Mubarak was faced by an Islamic fundamentalist terror campaign in the early 1990s. This targeted tourists and the police force and took several years to subdue, during which the police used heavy-handed tactics, especially in the south. Further liberalization of the economy created a boom in the late 1990s, but this growth has almost halted in the first years of the new millennium.

In 2005, Mubarak launched a series of political reforms culminating in Egypt's first-ever presidential elections, which took place later that year, and which he won resoundingly. In the following parliamentary elections, many members of the officially banned Muslim Brotherhood won seats. But political opponents criticize the many restrictions that remain, and consider the recent increase in freedoms to be far from secure. The growing internal opposition—from different points of the political spectrum, including Islamists, liberals, and leftists, all calling for true democracy and greater political reform—regards the reforms as cosmetic, aimed solely at easing a transfer of power within the regime.

GOVERNMENT AND POLITICS

Egypt has all the attributes of a democratic government: a constitution, three separate branches of government, a multiparty system, and most recently multicandidate elections. But, in reality, much of the power rests in the executive branch. Egypt has been living under a state of emergency almost continuously since 1967, via a law that gives extra powers to the executive, limits nongovernmental political activity, and curbs free speech in the name of national security. The emergency law, which must be renewed every three years, is due to be replaced with new antiterrorism legislation.

According to its constitution, Egypt is a democratic socialist republic. The Egyptian constitution states that all citizens are equal before the law with no discrimination on the grounds of race or religion. Egyptians are allowed to vote at the age of eighteen.

Egypt has a multiparty system. Currently there are more than twenty parties, though only five play a significant role in the political system. The current ruling party is the  National Democratic Party (NDP), which has been in power since 1978.

The Executive

The president of the republic is the head of state. The constitution grants wide powers to the executive, which is allowed to appoint the prime minister and one or more vice presidents. The cabinet is headed by the prime minister. The ministers of the interior, defense, and foreign affairs are appointed by the president himself. The president is also the commander of the armed forces and the head of the police.

Until 2005, a president had to be nominated by one-third of parliament and approved by two-thirds in a "yes–no" referendum. In 2005, President Mubarak proposed an amendment to the constitution to allow for multicandidate elections, which was approved by a referendum in May 2005. Subsequently, in Egypt's first-ever multicandidate elections, Mubarak won with

88 percent of the vote. In power since 1981, he is currently serving his fifth six-year term. Egypt's next presidential elections are due in 2011.

The Legislature

The legislature is made up of Egypt's parliament, the People's Assembly, or Magles el Sha'b, and the Advisory Council, Magles el Shura.

The People's Assembly seats 454 members; of these, ten are appointed by the president and 444 are elected. It is elected for a five-year term and must approve legislation and the program of the cabinet. The Advisory Council acts on a consultative basis.

The 2005 parliamentary elections saw the surprise success of the Muslim Brotherhood. Though officially banned, it fielded candidates as independents and won a staggering 20 percent of the seats. President Mubarak's ruling party, the NDP, still retains a majority, though it lost ninety-three seats from the previous year.

The Judiciary

The judiciary is independent of other authorities in theory, though the minister of justice is a cabinet member. The Egyptian legal system is derived primarily from the Napoleonic Code and personal status laws are dictated by Islamic law, *shari'a*. The Copts in Egypt are subject to their own personal status system. Egypt's highest court is the Supreme Constitutional Court.

Egypt distinguishes between criminal and civil courts. There are four types of court: tribunals, tribunals of the first instance, courts of appeal, and the Court of Cassation, which deals with further appeals on points of law. The Conseil d'Etat is a separate body that hears administrative disputes involving the government.

Foreign Relations

Egypt, a key mediator in the Middle East, has taken an active role in negotiations and diplomatic efforts between the Palestinians and the Israelis. It is on friendly terms with the U.S.A. and since the Camp David treaty of 1979 has had bilateral relations with Israel.

THE ECONOMY

Nasser's economic policy was shaped by import substitution, agricultural reform, and industrialization. Government investment was at the top of the agenda, and until 1970 most sectors of the economy were state owned. Sadat's Open Door Policy changed the economic landscape.

Economic reforms in 1991 reduced tariffs and customs in an attempt to continue the drive toward a market economy. A privatization program was launched. New monetary policies reduced inflation and decreased budget deficits. In 2004, the prime minister Ahmed Nazif introduced new business legislation and trimmed bureaucratic procedure to help encourage private and foreign investment. Egypt has been a member of the International Monetary Fund since 1945.

But, despite the reforms, Egypt is still considered a poor country. Overpopulation has put a significant strain on resources such as land and water. The economy relies on foreign aid and remittances from overseas workers: Egypt is the second-largest recipient of aid from the U.S.A.

Industry
Today major manufacturing plants are located in Cairo, Alexandria, Port Said, and Suez. Egypt's industry includes iron and steel, textiles, chemicals, cement, sugar, and cotton.

Egypt produces a significant amount of petroleum, though small by Middle East standards. Natural gas deposits have been located. Minerals found in Egypt are phosphates, salt, iron ore, manganese, limestone, gypsum, and gold.

Agriculture
Agriculture brings in about 18 percent of the GNP. Egypt's farmland is heavily cultivated. The Aswan Dam, completed in 1970, was intended to

control the annual floods and to generate electricity. It has enabled more land to be used for agriculture, but has also reduced the amount of nutrient-rich silt coming from Upper Egypt.

A large percentage of the labor force is employed in farming. Egypt's main crop is cotton. Other crops are maize, wheat, broad beans, sugar cane, onions, rice, potatoes, and citrus fruit. Egypt imports approximately half its food.

Egypt also imports chemical and mineral products, transport equipment, foodstuffs and consumer goods. Exports consist of petroleum, raw cotton (it is the world's largest exporter of cotton), textiles, and some agricultural crops.

Tourism
Tourism is a pillar of the economy. Egypt relies on it for 25 percent of its foreign currency revenue and approximately 6 percent of GNP. Terrorist threats have had a negative effect on the tourist industry but the government has taken strong measures to help the sector recuperate.

chapter two

VALUES &
ATTITUDES

Arab culture in general places great importance
on social harmony. People are more important
than time or money, and good personal relations
are at the core of the Egyptian value system.

One value that all Arabs share is the awareness
of dignity. Maintaining a person's dignity involves
not putting them on the spot, and not causing
them embarrassment. Hard sales tactics, for
example, are not popular in the Arab world: they
are considered rude and aggressive. When making
a request himself, an Egyptian tries to leave the
door open by not asking for an immediate
answer. It is all about saving face.

It is considered more polite to say, "I'll try to
come," than to say, "no," or "I can't come." When an
Egyptian is asked for something, he feels a sense
of duty to try to oblige. He will make a real effort
not to refuse a request directly, and to suppress
annoyed or angry reactions. If asked directions in
the street, and he doesn't know the answer, he will
often rather guess than say he can't help, even if it
would actually have been more helpful if he had

simply said, "I don't know." On the other hand, the general helpfulness of Egyptians, especially to foreigners, is the plus side of the same coin.

The day-to-day running of affairs may seem haphazard and random. Appointments and commitments are looser than in the West. Remember, time is not money. Being late for an appointment is not the end of the world, nor does it mean the end of a business deal. Promises are made easily, though not always fulfilled.

"IBM"

Egyptians realize that their attitude to times, dates, and appointments is vague. They laugh about it and call it the IBM syndrome: *Insha'allah* (God willing), *Bukra* (tomorrow), *Ma'lesh* (never mind!).

The Egyptians are friendly, cheerful, hospitable, and renowned for their sense of humor. Most of them endure difficult living conditions on a daily basis. Many need to juggle several jobs in order to make a decent enough income but, despite this, they seem to accept the cards they have been dealt with little fuss. They are deeply religious, and believe in the concept of an afterlife, working hard in this life and hoping to reap the benefits in the

next. They deal with problems by saying it is the
will of God. This calmness, sometimes interpreted
as indifference, is merely a survival tactic.

That is not to say that Egyptians are docile.
While they will make great efforts to maintain
someone else's dignity, if they feel insulted
tempers will flare. For example, if a man's wife has
been harassed, he cannot ignore it, and may well
get into a fistfight over the issue. He will do what
it takes to restore his pride.

STATUS AND SOCIAL STRUCTURE

From the 1940s until the Revolution of 1952,
population growth, the spread of education,
industrialization, and the migration from rural to
urban areas all allowed for a degree of social
mobility. Despite this, there existed a clear
division between the wealthy landowning class
and the peasants. A small professional class was
recruited mainly from the peasant class.

The 1952 Revolution paved the way for drastic
changes in the class system. The new socialist
ideology meant that breaking through class
barriers was no longer an impossible goal. There
were two main routes to upward mobility:
education, or a career in the army. The Nasser
years saw the expansion of a professional middle
class and the creation of an industrial working

class. The post-Revolution years also gave birth to a new military class. Eventually, status was no longer associated with wealth and land but with power and connections with the regime.

After Nasser's death in 1970, Sadat replaced the socialist economic system with laissez-faire capitalism. His market-directed Open Door Policy enabled many entrepreneurs, and opportunists, to make money and paved the way for the growth of a new wealthy middle class.

Upward mobility continues to this day; consequently the class structure is ambiguous. Today Egyptian society is loosely divided into three groups: an extremely wealthy class that is powerful through connections and money; the mass of Egyptians, who are extremely poor; and a small professional and middle class, which is educated. While the class system is not as institutionalized as in other parts of the world, Egyptian society is very class-based. People instinctively work and socialize within their own class. Social gaps exist between rich and poor, educated and illiterate, urban and rural.

The wealthy have adopted many of the values of Western society; they dress and behave in a similar fashion. They carry laptops and iPods, and wear designer clothes. The rest of society is largely conservative; it holds to traditional values, where family and religion play central roles.

Another clear division in Egyptian society is the urban–rural divide. Upper-class urbanites regard rural people as backward; in their daily vocabulary, the word *fellah* (peasant) is derogatory. Meanwhile, some from rural towns see the city people as loose and degenerate.

In the countryside the class structure is similar. While old family names still matter in the villages, status has also become connected with power. Some, especially if connected to the regime, enjoy more power and privileges than others.

Being a *Muwazaff*

When Nasser was in power, he instituted a system whereby any university graduate was guaranteed a job for life in the public sector. Being a *muwazaff* (a government employee) was a status symbol. The lifelong job with a pension and benefits allowed people to buy items on credit or in installments and artificially raised living standards. But the growing population caused problems for the government, which had to find employment for graduates when vacancies no longer existed. As a result, the public sector became saturated and several people were hired to perform the job of one person. Today the desire for the title of *muwazzaf* still exists, particularly in rural Egypt, even though the government can no longer guarantee these jobs. This means that the young often turn down work in the private sector, awaiting that coveted government position. A large portion of the workforce is thus put on hold, the government cannot keep up, and a backlog of unemployment is being created.

EGYPTIAN PRIDE

Though Egypt's contribution to the world has dwindled significantly since its last period of glory in the Middle Ages, modern Egyptians are a proud people. Egypt industrialized in the nineteenth century, well ahead of other Arab countries, and the population constitutes almost one-third of all the Arabs. Egyptians are proud of their heritage and of their position as cultural and political leaders of the Arab world. They often tend to be dismissive of other Arab countries.

This is not to say that they are not well aware of their own problems. The rampant poverty, the overcrowding, and continued unemployment make life difficult for the great majority. This, however, is information they will rarely share with foreigners as they are eager to portray the positive side of their country. Speaking negatively about your country in front of a foreigner is equal to washing your dirty linen in public. Two Egyptians having coffee together might criticize their society or government but, as soon as a foreigner walks in, they will stop. In fact, if a foreigner wants to hear an Egyptian's honest opinion of Egypt, he or she must compliment the place.

SOCIAL NETWORKS

This is a society where the group is more significant than the individual. There are no single-portion meals in supermarkets, nor do people go to the cinema alone. Studio apartments are few and many houses are full of family.

Social obligations are at the heart of social interaction. If someone is ill, family and friends must go to see them. Likewise, when someone returns from a trip, family and friends will visit them to welcome them back. Friends and relatives call on newlywed couples in their marital abode to congratulate them. A new mother must be visited with gifts for the baby soon after the birth.

One of the biggest fears Egyptians have is of being alone. A wife whose husband goes away on a business trip will often stay with her mother for the duration; a widowed parent will move in with the children. Being on your own is considered a sad state and your social networks, family, neighbors, and friends are there to protect you from exactly that. Friends and family crowd round on special occasions and in times of crisis.

The family is the most important social unit in Egypt. Family ties are very strong: Egyptians receive moral as well as financial support from the family and are expected to give it priority.

Egyptians have many acquaintances, and wide social networks. Real friendship, however, comes with commitments. It is essential to keep friendships alive by visiting often and asking after friends regularly. Neighbors play a role too: they are immediate candidates for friendship. In the older buildings, where families have passed apartments on through the generations, neighbors are close and are a point of call in an emergency. Neighbors in the poorer areas are on especially intimate terms as they need to pool their resources far more.

Social networks are used in business and in day-to-day affairs. The personal dimension plays a part in every aspect of life. Recommendations take one much further than a good résumé. It is all about contacts. For example, an Egyptian is unlikely to use a directory to find a plumber, who is usually recommended by someone you know. And a plumber, on his part, will make you a priority if you were mentioned by a client of his.

RELIGION

Islam is the official religion of Egypt, and approximately 90 percent of the population is Sunni Muslim. Apart from tiny Jewish, Shi'i

Muslim, and Baha'i communities, the rest of the population is Christian, most belonging to the Coptic Orthodox Church.

Coptic Christianity

One of the world's oldest Christian communities, the Copts are descended from those ancient

Egyptians who embraced Christianity in the first century. Coptic, a member of the Hamito-Semitic language group, is the ritual language of the Coptic Church. It is written in the Greek alphabet with some additional letters. The Coptic Church is headed by the pope of Alexandria.

On the surface, Egyptian Copts are indistinguishable from Egyptian Muslims. They share the same value systems and mix in the same circles. Egyptian Copts are very religious. Every area has a large church that families attend. Each family chooses a priest for confession, and he also fulfills the role of family counselor.

Islam

Islam defines not only one's relationship with God, but also all interpersonal relations and daily life. In Egypt Islam is visible, audible, and tangible. The call to prayer resounds from every mosque five times a day, and verses of the Qur'an are framed and hung on the walls of houses.

Fate plays an important role in popular Islam. This concept underlines the belief that everything that happens in one's life is the will of God. Among Egypt's largely uneducated lower classes, Islam is intertwined with various practices contrary to accepted orthodox belief, like the reverence of saints, the use of magic, and the conduct of pagan rituals.

There are five duties that need to be carried out during a Muslim's life: the declaration of faith, prayer, charity, fasting, and pilgrimage.

Islam's holy book, the Qur'an, is considered by Muslims to be the word of God as dictated to the Prophet Mohammed by the angel Gabriel during the month of Ramadan. The Qur'an is made up of 114 chapters, each called a *sura*, divided into verses called *aya*. It addresses codes of behavior, society, and law. After the Qur'an was received by Mohammed, there was a huge effort to preserve it

faithfully, so priority was given to learning the text by heart. It is the primary theological source of Islam. The interpretation of the Qur'an, in theory at least, is constantly evolving and is studied by Islamic theologians to this day.

The second source, the *hadith*, is the collection of the Prophet's sayings and actions, used to complement the Qur'an as a source of religious and legal guidance for the Muslim community. The *hadith* was eventually codified.

Although Muslims agree on the basic rules of Islam, the various social groups apply religion differently in their daily lives. The rural and lower-middle classes tend to be more observant. The affluent who have adopted Western ways consider themselves believers, often guiltily regarding their lifestyle (if it involves drinking and dating freely) as wrong. It is extremely rare to find an Egyptian who is openly agnostic or atheist. It is, in fact, considered highly offensive for someone to say they do not believe in God.

Mosques

Cairo is sometimes referred to as "the city of a thousand minarets." Mosques date back to the earliest times in Islam, and were then constructed

through the Abbasid, Fatimid, Mamluk, and Ottoman periods to the modern day, with a matching range of architectural styles. If you wish to visit a mosque in Egypt, there are certain guidelines and rules to be observed. Note that non-Muslims are not allowed in at prayer time.

- Wear modest clothing. Nobody should wear shorts or short-sleeved T-shirts. Women should cover their hair (some mosques provide scarves at the entrance), and should be covered except for face, hands, and feet. Loose trousers or long skirts are appropriate, and long, loose shirts. Avoid anything that outlines the contours of the body.
- There are separate entrances for men and women. Leave your shoes at the entrance.
- You sit on the floor in a mosque, but chairs can be provided for pregnant women and the disabled. Don't lie stretched out on the floor.
- All the general rules of public decorum apply, only more strictly. It is important not to step in front of anyone who is praying.

ATTITUDES TOWARD WOMEN

In recent decades there have been radical changes in the situation of women in education and employment. During the 1960s, the number of women in the labor force grew. In 2003, Egypt appointed a female judge to the High Constitutional Court for the first time. Recently there have been major reforms to the legal status of women. Despite this, gender inequality still exists in Egyptian society.

The gender gap is most evident in the rural areas. Economic pressures on poorer families force many parents to withdraw their children from school in order to help earn the family's income. Generally it is the daughters who are pulled out of schools first. Many women eventually find jobs in the informal sector.

In Egypt, the law does not discriminate between men and women regarding pay. But society still puts pressure on women to take on less demanding jobs as their primary duty should be to the home. Despite this, many upper- and middle-class women are professionals who juggle work and family. Among the working and rural classes, the the ideal role for a woman is that of "homemaker." In this context, a woman's status is measured by her husband's wealth and the amount of domestic help she receives.

A family's honor depends very much on the reputation of its women, which, if tarnished, can damage its social standing. A woman is expected to be a virgin on her wedding day; premarital sex is an absolute taboo (though of course it may take place discreetly). For this reason, families tend to be stricter with girls than with boys.

The personal status of women is derived from Islamic law, or *shari'a*, which outlines the rules for marriage, divorce, and inheritance. According to Islamic law, polygamy is allowed: a man may take up to four wives, although this rarely happens, for practical reasons. In 2000, the Egyptian parliament revised the Personal Status Law to provide women with more rights. In Islam, a man can obtain a divorce without the wife's consent. For a woman to obtain a divorce, the burden of proof fell on her to give evidence of wrongdoing. The process usually dragged women through the courts and the lengthy procedure deterred many women from initiating proceedings. This recent amendment allows women to obtain a divorce quite easily on condition that the husband is exempt from any financial obligations.

The rise of Islamist movements has also reinforced traditional gender roles. Women are seen as symbols of the family—keepers of cultural values and traditions, and teachers of the next generation. The adoption of the *higab* (a head scarf rather than a full face veil) is the most visible expression of the rising religious sentiment. Today most Egyptian Muslim women wear the *higab*.

"*INSHA'ALLAH*"

Egyptians are fatalistic and superstitious. Good fortune is God's mercy, and misfortune is His will. The submission to God is even evident in daily speech. The expression "*insha'allah*" means "if God wills." Egyptians inject this expression into every sentence that denotes intention; not to use it is seen as tempting fate.

Therefore, if talking in the future tense, the word *insha'allah* must be used. An Egyptian will never say, "I'm going to Alexandria tomorrow;" he will most definitely say, "I'm going to Alexandria tomorrow *insha'allah*." The final decision is that of God. If one forgets to say *insha'allah*, someone else will interject with a reminder. For example, if someone asks, "Are you going to Alexandria tomorrow," and the reply is "Yes," the person who asked will often add the missing *insha'allah*.

Today, in practice, the use of the word has increased tremendously. It has become the easiest and most noncommittal answer to a question, and might mean, "yes," "probably," "probably not," and "no." It has reached absurd proportions whereby you can ask someone, "Have you finished this task?" and they will reply *insha'allah*, even if they have finished it! The use of *insha'allah* confuses and frustrates many foreigners.

BACKHAND ECONOMY

Rigid state bureaucracy, a poor educational system, and low wages have allowed corruption to flourish and the sense of social responsibility to diminish. Many Egyptians bend the rules without compunction because they feel that the top strata of society are far more corrupt. The mass of the poor know that they have little power within the system and tend to think that, since they can't change the status quo, there is no point in making huge personal efforts for little in return.

The average Egyptian will face, on a regular basis, bureaucratic obstacles caused by badly thought-out procedures, or artificially created by state officials looking for a bribe. Sometimes the only way forward is by oiling the wheels. Bribes are often offered as small exchanges, perhaps to speed up the renewal of a driver's license, to get a new copy of a passport, or as a sweetener to a traffic policeman to avoid a parking ticket.

WASTA

The support system that Egyptians rely on is provided by their social network, including family, friends, and acquaintances. This has become even more important, especially within the context of an increasingly unpredictable and corrupt state system. Calling old friends for "favors" and pulling strings is now the norm.

Wasta (connections) is the key to getting a good job, sometimes even any job. This means you need to keep alive the contacts you have. Family is usually the first point of call but might not have all the necessary connections, so people use friends or acquaintances, depending on their needs. The other side of the coin is that, using *wasta*, people can end up with jobs they are unqualified for. It is often not about what you know but who you know.

The underprivileged class in Egypt, those unlikely to have a strong *wasta*, will often approach figures of authority with an attitude of caution and perhaps even sycophancy.

TOLERANCE AND PREJUDICE

Though conservative in their own society, Egyptians are quite tolerant of Westerners' "strange" customs and generally expect foreigners to be different. There are, however, things that are simply not tolerated.

Homosexuality, for example, is not accepted by Muslims or Christians on either religious or social grounds. Though there is a homosexual community in Egypt, they usually live a secret life and only reveal their sexuality to close, liberal-minded friends who will not ostracize them. Displays of romantic, sexual affection between two men are not tolerated, and are likely to result in hostility and possibly violence.

Neither are open displays of affection by heterosexual couples acceptable. Kissing on the street will attract a great deal of attention and offend those nearby.

Unfortunately, as in most developing societies, the world's population is usually categorized according to a cultural–racial hierarchy. White Westerners are at the top, Egyptians next, then Arabs, followed by Asians, and lastly Africans. While these attitudes are undoubtedly racist, they do not find violent expression toward poorer local Sudanese, for instance. Such racism is at most confined to derogatory comments and/or ridicule. With the police it could be a different matter, but then they deal violently with the poorer classes of Egyptian as well.

SENSE OF HUMOR

Centuries of occupation, oppression, and economic hardship have given Egyptians a vital means of self-preservation: a sense of humor. Even religion is the subject of jest, within limits. To measure the importance of an event, you count how many jokes have been made about it.

Egyptians make fun of social relations, local politics, foreigners, and themselves. Upper (southern) Egyptians, stereotypically tough, stubborn, and stupid, are the butt of many jokes.

CUSTOMS & TRADITIONS

In Egypt customs and tradition play a central role in people's lives. Though most customs have a religious origin, it is their social function that glues society together.

CALENDARS

In Egypt both the Christian (Gregorian and Coptic) and the Islamic calendars are used. Business generally uses the Gregorian, while religious holidays are dictated by the religious calendars.

The Islamic calendar is based on the phases of the moon and consists of twelve lunar months. The lunar year is 354 days long, so the dates move in relation to the Gregorian calendar. The calendar begins with the Prophet Mohammed's migration from Mecca to Medina in the year 622 CE of the Gregorian calendar.

The Coptic Calendar

There are thirteen months in the Coptic calendar: twelve have thirty days each and the last month five or six days depending on whether it is a leap year. This calendar is used today not just by Copts in a religious context, but by all Egyptians. Weather, and agricultural seasons and harvests are referred to using the Coptic calendar. All Egyptians calculate the period of the Khamasin (the annual southerly winds and sandstorms) by it.

RAMADAN

Ramadan, the ninth month of the lunar Muslim calendar, is when the Qur'an was said to have been revealed to the Prophet Mohammed. During this month adult Muslims fast—they abstain from eating, drinking, and sex, from sunrise to sunset. The elderly, sick, and pregnant are exempt.

Ramadan is a huge event in Egypt. A festive spirit sweeps the country, decorations adorn the streets, households prepare for the event in advance, and business hours are altered to accommodate the fasters.

Traditionally, people had to wait for the crescent moon to be observed before the fast was declared. Today, the start date of a lunar month is of course known in advance, but the tradition of spotting the moon has been upheld. In the old days there would be a procession to a site where the

moon could be seen clearly, and lanterns were used to light the way. Today these have evolved into elaborate decorations hung outside homes, in the streets, and in the shops; during Ramadan children are customarily given a colorful lantern.

On the first day of Ramadan, people usually break the fast with their families. The *iftar* (the breaking of the fast) is a ceremonious affair that takes a lot of preparation. People wait for the sunset call to prayer before they begin to eat. It was said that the Prophet used to break his fast with a few dates and a glass of milk. Today many people like to keep up this tradition. The *iftar* usually consists of a soup and several dishes of meat, rice or pasta, and vegetables.

After the *iftar*, families take their tea and dessert around the television as they watch the array of programs made especially for Ramadan. The guaranteed audience means that most production companies pour the largest chunk of their budgets into soap operas screened during Ramadan. Actors' celebrity is measured by appearances at this time. Advertising companies reserve large proportions of their money, creativity, and talent for Ramadan advertising.

Charity and goodwill are important principles in Ramadan. For this reason, it is common for people who have not made it home at *iftar* time to be handed a date or fruit by a stranger. Outside mosques, long wooden or plastic tables are laid out with a simple *iftar* free of charge for those who are fasting and have nowhere to eat. Even away from mosques, one can see these tables, known as *mawa'id el rahman* (tables of the Merciful) all around the country, set up by wealthy people for those in need. Beggars and street sweepers often line up to get a place at one throughout the month. Even a person who can afford his own *iftar* but has not made it home on time will be welcome: the idea is that no one should be alone during *iftar*. The *mawa'id el rahman* should not, however, be treated merely as an interesting cultural experience, and foreigners who are not fasting should not sit at one.

The *suhur* is the last meal of the day during Ramadan and usually takes place shortly before sunrise, when the next day's fasting begins. It usually consists of *ful* (Egyptian beans), cheese, eggs, yogurt, or any light meal.

In the big cities, the *suhur* has evolved from a necessary meal to a large-scale commercial affair. Today, hotels, companies, and individuals set up Ramadan tents, big marquees that offer a set menu, music, and some form of live entertainment. These range in price and opulence. Some of the larger ones provide a rich program in lavish surroundings and sometimes a *wasta* is needed to get in.

With all the spirituality and festivity that sweeps the country at Ramadan, there is also an air of tension in the first few days when people are still adjusting to not eating and drinking. The fasting itself can be difficult, particularly when Ramadan falls in summer: the weather is hot and the days are long. Tempers can flare as people, especially coffee drinkers and smokers, suffer from their respective withdrawal symptoms.

Cairo, which is notorious for its traffic jams, becomes a series of gridlocks as everyone rushes home from work to join friends and family for the *iftar*. Most businesses will devote one day of the month to a company *iftar* at a restaurant.

Foreigners, while not expected to fast, should respect the spirit of Ramadan. It is rude to eat or drink in the street while others are fasting. Most cafés and restaurants will still be open, so eating and drinking can be done discreetly indoors.

Because it is a sacred month, you will find that most Egyptians dress more modestly during Ramadan. For the same reason, people who drink alcohol during the year stop during this month.

OTHER RELIGIOUS HOLIDAYS
Islamic New Year
Muharram is the first month of the Islamic calendar. There is no public celebration, though usually government and religious officials mark it with a special function. It is a national holiday.

Prophet Mohammed's Birthday

Mulid el Nabi is a national holiday. It is mainly a family celebration. Children are decked out in their best clothes and given special sweets, in particular *'aruset el mulid*, in the shape of a girl dressed in a big gown, all made of sugar.

Eid el Fitr

Eid el Fitr (*eid* means feast and *fitr* breaking of the fast) is the three-day feast that marks the end of Ramadan. On the first day men traditionally head to their local mosque for the communal Eid prayer at sunrise. People greet each other by saying "*Eid Mubarak*" ("Blessed Eid"). A very important aspect of Eid is charity and all Muslims who are able are expected to give to the needy.

Eid festivities take place more in the home than on the street. It is a time for family. Customarily, after the Eid prayer, families will go for a large celebratory lunch, usually at the home of one of the older members. Children are given cash and new clothes. Special sweet shortbread biscuits (*kahk*) are offered to guests.

Eid el Adha

Eid el Adha (feast of the sacrifice) is perhaps the most sacred of Muslim festivals, a celebration to mark the pilgrimage to Mecca. A four-day feast commemorates the story of Abraham, who was tested by being asked to sacrifice his son. In the Bible the son is Isaac, in the Qur'an it is Ismail. Muslims offer a sacrifice of their own by slaughtering an animal and donating most of the meat to the poor.

After prayer, families gather at home to have a hearty breakfast of *fatta*, a dish made of meat, bread, and rice, topped with vinegar and garlic

Coptic Christmas

Coptic Christmas is celebrated on January 7. In 2002, this was declared an official national holiday as a sign of Muslim–Christian unity.

On Christmas Eve, Copts attend the mass at church before gathering in their homes for a turkey dinner. The biggest Nativity service is held in Cairo's Cathedral of St. Mark. A type of bread, called *qurban*, is distributed after the service; it is round, decorated with a cross and has twelve dots representing the disciples of Jesus. On Christmas Day itself, gifts are exchanged. Copts make special sweet biscuits for Christmas, similar to *kahk*.

Shamm el Nessim

Egyptians have been celebrating Sham el Nessim, the feast marking the arrival of spring, for 4,500 years. In Ancient Egypt the harvest season was known as *Shamo*. In Arabic, *shamm* means to smell and *nessim* means breeze, so in Arabic the feast is known as the "smelling of the breeze."

The Ancient Egyptians used to celebrate the beginning of spring by offering salted fish (*fiseekh*), lettuce, and eggs to their deities. The lettuce was said to represent the start of spring; the eggs renewal of life, and the fish fertility. Today, though considered by many as a pagan holiday, Shamm el Nessim is still celebrated in Egypt by most people of all faiths, who eat the same combination of foods. The eggs are dyed and decorated with colorful designs, much like Easter eggs in many Christian countries.

Because Shamm el Nessim comes before the summer heat sets in, it is celebrated outdoors. Millions of Egyptians take over the parks and other green spaces to "smell the breeze."

NATIONAL HOLIDAYS
Sinai Liberation Day (April 25)
Sinai Liberation day marks the end of the Israeli occupation of the Sinai Peninsula. Sinai was fully returned to Egypt and the Egyptian flag was raised on the Peninsula on April 25, 1982.
Labor Day (May 1)
Liberation Day (June 18)
This commemorates the departure of the last British troops from Egypt in 1956, ending an occupation that had lasted seventy-four years. There are celebrations in schools and universities.

Revolution Day (July 23)
July 23, 1952 is the day the Free Officers, led by a young Gamal Abd-al Nasser, toppled the Egyptian monarchy in a military coup. The puppet king was deposed and the Egyptian republic was born.

Armed Forces Day (October 6)
The celebration of the Egyptian army's crossing into Sinai in 1973 and its victory over the Israeli forces.

Suez Victory Day (October 24)
This marks the day in 1973 when the port of Suez resisted Israeli air and ground attacks. Residents burned Israeli tanks at the entrance to the city.

Victory Day (December 23)
This celebration takes place mainly in Port Said. It is a commemoration of Egypt's victory over the British, French, and Israelis in 1956.

OTHER CELEBRATIONS
Christmas Day (December 25) and New Year's Day (January 1)
While these are not traditional Egyptian celebrations, today they are popular among the affluent classes. Western (as distinct from Coptic) Christmas is becoming more noticeable in the large cities. It used to be celebrated mainly by the small Catholic community, but it is now fashionable for Westernized Egyptians to get

Christmas trees. Street vendors sell Christmas hats at traffic lights and the streets are decorated, especially in areas with foreign residents.

New Year's Eve sees all the five-star hotels booked up with fancy parties, bursting with drinks, entertainment, hats, and poppers.

Mother's Day (March 21)

This is not a public holiday, but is celebrated by Egyptians of all faiths and classes. Children give their mothers gifts or cards, and television stations broadcast special programs.

MULIDS

A *mulid* (literally, "birthday") is the celebration of a saint, a custom observed by both Muslims and Christians. Sanctification of a person is forbidden according to a strict interpretation of Islam, and some consider these fairs sacrilegious. But the tradition is popular throughout the country, especially in the rural areas and among the poor. *Mulid* season starts in May and ends in October.

Mulids are vibrant events, bursting with color and festivity. Most villages and every large city area have their own saint whose festival is celebrated once a year. Swings for children, drinking areas for the adults, and booths selling toys are erected. There is singing and dancing, and entertainment, often in brightly colored tents with illuminations.

A professional group of people called the *mawaldiya* generally organize *mulids* and other occasions. They set it up, dismantle it when it's over, and head off to the next saint's location.

Mulids are sacred events for members of the Sufi order, the mystical branch of Islam. Their sheikhs dress in colorful robes, while "whirling dervishes" perform their spellbinding routine. Others perform the *zikr*, chanting religious songs to hypnotic rhythms that lead to a state of trance. The atmosphere is alive with incense, music, and prayer.

SUPERSTITION

People from all segments of society are generally superstitious. They believe that if someone is envious of you they can cause your good luck to disappear by casting the evil eye on you. For this reason, Egyptians can be quite discreet about good things. They may not reveal a new job until the start date, or talk about a salary raise. There are certain ways to ward off the evil eye, like burning incense, using a protective blue bead, or reading certain verses of the Qur'an.

A new house is blessed with a mixture of frankincense and Arabic gum called *bukhoor*. A new baby may wear a little brooch with a blue bead on it. A new car is likely to have a copy of the Qur'an placed in it somewhere.

If someone pays a compliment, they must say the words *masha'allah* afterward to show that their intentions are good and that they are not trying to put the evil eye on something. Thus, when admiring someone's new home, you must say "*masha'allah*, what a lovely house."

When a person comes into some good fortune, they must share it with others, otherwise it is believed their luck will run out. If someone buys a new home, for example, they must slaughter an animal and give the meat to the poor.

In Egypt, owls and black cats are considered bad omens, and bearers of bad news. Egyptians won't leave shoes upside down because it is said that the sole of the shoe should not face God. Open scissors are a sign of bad luck.

Nothing should be placed on top of a copy of the Qur'an.

chapter four

MAKING FRIENDS

Because Egyptians are friendly and hospitable, acquaintances are easy to make. Meet one Egyptian and you are likely very quickly to meet his extended social network. But deep friendships are acquired through repeated interaction over time. Egyptians put a lot of time and effort into developing friendships, from which they expect trust and commitment. Wrongdoing may be forgiven simply because the two parties have known each other for so long. They will often refer to *el 'ishra*, the long time spent together.

The Westernized upper classes, a tiny minority, socialize in a similar fashion to the West. Men and women mix freely; dating is not uncommon. They go to parties, mingle at bars, and take weekend trips to the desert or beach resorts.

The vast majority of the population, especially in rural areas, is generally more conservative; most socializing takes place in a family setting. Families visit each other frequently and their children get to know each other from an early age. In the cities, many friendships are cultivated at school or at university and people will often socialize with the same group for years. Male–female friendships are not common.

Though the rules for Egyptian–Egyptian friendships may be rigid—people instinctively mix with their own social class and tight networks can be difficult to break into—with foreigners the rules are more relaxed. Egyptians are very open to foreigners; in fact they will make double the effort to ensure their foreign friends feel welcome.

Egyptians are generous and will happily invite friends for meals, buy them gifts, and offer their time. They do this in the knowledge that real friendships are long-term and gestures of kindness and hospitality are reciprocated, even if not immediately.

Society imposes stricter rules for girls than for boys. Particularly in the rural and poorer classes, it is common for boys to socialize outside the house in groups but girls are often housebound. When girls are allowed to go out, they are usually subject to strict parent-imposed curfews.

ATTITUDES TO FOREIGNERS

Most foreigners visiting Egypt are tourists, and Egyptians are used to the idea of them coming

and going without making any long-term
friendships locally. Egyptians are gracious and
hospitable, however, and a foreigner who shows
respect for their culture is warmly embraced.

Wealthy, urban Egyptians are the most likely to
be well traveled or educated abroad. They relate to
foreigners easily and can quickly make friends
with them. The less educated Egyptians often have
misguided perceptions of foreigners. Their main
window into the lifestyle and behavior of
foreigners is via the mass media, particularly
television and more specifically soap operas and
music videos. To them, life abroad resembles
Universal Studios and is deeply coveted by many
youngsters, frustrated by their lives at home.

Television series such as Dallas and Falcon
Crest have shaped the image of Western women
and their relations with the opposite sex in the
minds of many Egyptian males. And therefore the
sometimes provocative dress and open behavior
of some foreign women can be misinterpreted by
Egyptian men as a sign of sexual availability.

Egyptians call Western foreigners *khawagas*.
While many traditional Egyptians see *khawagas* as
materially and perhaps intellectually advanced,
they also regard them as morally inferior.
Egyptians are often appalled by the fact that, in
the West, children move out of their homes before

getting married, or parents can be sent to nursing homes. To them, this represents a lack of family values. This does not mean that Egyptians are not open to relationships with *khawagas*. But the key is respect for the culture. Egyptians will cherish a foreigner who does not flaunt his, or her, own ways or try to "educate" them but rather appreciates Egyptian attitudes and customs.

GREETINGS

Greetings are very important and many Egyptians will form their opinion of someone based on the way they greet them. Warmth is fundamental, even in formal settings. Egyptians make a distinction between formality and coldness. You can be formal but warm; for example, a firm handshake can be accompanied by a smile.

People of the same sex greet each other with affection. Women kiss on both cheeks when they meet. Sometimes, especially in the rural areas, they kiss more than once on each cheek, and may kiss the hand of an elderly relative to show respect.

Men who know each other well also kiss each other on both cheeks. A pat on the back is an extra sign of warmth. Handshakes between men need to be strong and firm, as limp handshakes are considered insincere. It is also quite common to see men walking hand-in-hand or arm-in-arm; it is no indication of their sexual orientation.

The rules are different for relations with the opposite sex, where minimal physical contact is the norm. A polite brief handshake is acceptable. A man should not extend his hand to a woman he does not know well; he should wait for her to extend her hand first. Public displays of affection are unacceptable, even between husband and wife.

It is rude to see an acquaintance and not greet them, even if they seem busy or are engaged in conversation with someone else. A distant wave is considered rude.

Verbal greetings, which can be rich and flowery, vary according to the situation. The most straightforward greeting when meeting someone or arriving at a place is *salamu 'aleiko*, which literally mean "peace be upon you." The reply to that would be *wa 'aleikom el salam*, "and peace be upon you." It is rude not to reply to that specific greeting even if it is not personally directed at you. Walk into any cinema and say *salamu 'aleiko* and the whole audience will break out into a chorus of *wa 'aleikom el salam*!

The standard morning greeting is *sabah el kheir*. Literally translated this means "morning of joy." In reply one can repeat *sabah el kheir* or, more warmly, *sabah el nur* ("morning of light").

HOSPITALITY

The Egyptians are masters of hospitality. If they think you may be dining alone, they may insist on inviting you home for dinner. They will insist on paying when out for dinner.

If dining out with an Egyptian who insists on paying the bill, the guest should also insist on paying. Most of the time, there will be a push and pull and it is the person with the strongest will who finally pays. If paid for, it is polite to return the invitation on a later occasion.

As in many Arab cultures, in Egypt the guest is revered. Particularly if they are foreign guests, Egyptians feel responsible for their well-being. They are genuinely concerned about the visitor's comfort and satisfaction with their trip, going out of their way to show the good side of Egypt.

It is rare to go to an Egyptian's house and not be served something to eat or drink and most probably both. Even if you arrive on short notice, it is highly likely that the host has something in the kitchen "just for guests."

INVITATIONS HOME

When invited to lunch or dinner at an Egyptian's home, it is polite to accept. The customary thing to bring is some dessert. There are numerous pastry shops where you can pick up a plate of

Arabic sweets or a cake for after dinner. Do not bring alcohol, unless you know the person very well and are certain that they drink. Flowers, while appreciated in certain Westernized homes, are considered useless by most Egyptians.

Egyptian women will go out of their way to put out a big spread for a guest. Lunch or dinner invitations are a time when the woman of the house can showcase her talents in the kitchen. Even in modest homes, you will rarely be invited for just a "pasta and salad."

Egyptians generally do not arrive on time. If a dinner invitation is set for 8:00 p.m., for example, it is customary to arrive fifteen or thirty minutes late. It is polite to wait for all the guests to arrive before serving the meal. The women of the house (wife and daughters) will be in the kitchen applying the final touches and will join the guests at the table. It is courteous for female guests to offer to help in the kitchen.

Meals are not served in courses. All the food is set in the middle of the table. When the meal is over, the hosts will lead the guests to the sitting area to have tea or coffee with the dessert.

In rural areas, it is customary for the hosts not to eat with the guests.

A table is prepared for the guests and the hosts disappear until they have finished eating. This is so that they can eat as much as they want without feeling shy.

At the end of the evening, Egyptians will walk their guests to the door; they never shut the front door before the guests are out of sight.

MANNERS

At the dining table, you should wait to be served. If you finish what's on your plate, you will be served again. If your plate is clear, it means that you are still hungry. Because women spend so much time in the kitchen preparing for their guests, it is polite to pay them a compliment. An appropriate phrase would be *sallim edeiki*, which means "bless your hands."

It is considered impolite to leave immediately after a meal. After coffee and dessert, you may gently start to introduce your good-byes.

Many Egyptian men smoke and they do so freely at most outings and in homes. In the more traditional households, a young man will not smoke in front of his father or an elder as a sign of respect. Women who do smoke generally do not do so in front of elders.

chapter five

PRIVATE & FAMILY LIFE

Until recently most of Egypt's population lived near agricultural land. About twenty years ago, as overpopulation resulted in scarcity of land, people began to migrate to the cities. Many have maintained their ties with their original villages, and to this day they return on special occasions.

In the cities, most housing consists of apartments, either in purpose-built blocks or in old, converted villas. Many old villas are being torn down in favor of large apartment blocks to accommodate the growing population. To escape overcrowding and pollution, the wealthy are moving into new housing developments that are mushrooming on the outskirts of the big cities. These gated compounds provide a safe and clean community space but they come at great expense.

The interior style in urban homes is eclectic, bringing together different cultural influences—Islamic, French, and Ottoman—and is jokingly referred to as "Louis Farouk." This is readily available: Egyptian carpenters and craftsmen have mastered the art of its elaborate woodwork.

Rural houses are built of mud or brick. Village furnishings are more rustic, with cushions or couches lining the walls in the space reserved for guests and family gatherings. Most homes have a television set, which provides the evening entertainment for the family.

THE HOUSEHOLD

In Egypt the most common and acceptable form of household is family based, with the father at the head. The household usually includes the nuclear family; it can consist of extended family, but rarely does it include nonrelatives. It is uncommon for individuals to live alone. Children move out of their parents' homes only to move into their new marital homes, and elderly parents move in with their children when they are no longer able to look after themselves.

In a traditional household, family roles are clearly defined. The father is the boss. He is the breadwinner and the decision maker and his rulings are hardly ever questioned. The wife's financial needs are covered by the husband and in return she is expected to take care of the domestic duties. This is the case even if she has an outside job. Along with her paid work, a woman shops, cleans, cooks, and looks after the children. Egyptian women are house-proud and care about their domestic reputation.

The eldest son usually takes over family responsibilities when the father reaches retirement age or is incapable of continuing. Traditionally, younger members of the family defer to older members, and women to men.

But Egyptian society is changing rapidly. Particularly in the middle and upper classes, women are increasingly free of this structure. They are more engaged in public life and may share the decision-making power and daily chores with their husbands.

GROWING UP IN EGYPT

Children have special status in Egyptian society: they are considered a blessing. They are loved and pampered first and disciplined when they are a little older. Egyptian mothers are well known to fuss over their children and see no wrong in them. An Egyptian expression highlights this well: *el ird fi 'ain ommo ghazal*, meaning "the monkey is a gazelle in his mother's eye."

The idea of babysitters is totally alien. If needed, family members are available for that type of support, but children are welcomed in most places and are often taken to restaurants, to cinemas, and to dinner at other people's homes.

It is normal for strangers to be affectionate and tactile with children. Don't be surprised if your child is whisked away by a cooing waitress at a restaurant or offered sweets by a stranger.

Life then becomes an uphill struggle for many children. The school years put enormous pressure on pupils and families. Children in full-time education in the public system have a lot of homework. Free time is filled with private lessons to compensate for a poor educational system. This puts a strain on families' pockets. Those attending secondary schools are subject to great pressure to pass their *thanawiyya 'amma*, the final exam.

If students make it to university and graduate, they are then faced with the reality of slim job prospects. Each year in Egypt 700,000 new graduates compete for about 200,000 jobs. Young people are frustrated as they end up working not in their chosen field, if they get work at all. This leads many to look for opportunities abroad.

On the social front, many middle-class children and young teenagers go to social clubs. Set up in the late nineteenth century for expatriate British families, these offered sports and recreational facilities, including tennis courts, swimming

pools, horse-riding, tea gardens, and so on.
Membership became open to Egyptians only in
the 1940s, and depended on status. After the
Revolution these clubs were nationalized and
membership was opened to all. Today they receive
money from the government and are run by the
Ministry of Youth and Sports. Children spend
much of their spare time in these clubs and
develop social networks that can last a lifetime.

European-style cafés have had a big social
impact. They are a favorite hangout for wealthy
teenagers, who meet there after school and on
weekends. They can spend hours sipping
capuccinos and lattes, watching music videos, and
smoking flavored water pipes (often behind their
parents' back!). In the evenings, girls generally
have earlier curfews than boys.

Education
The education system went through a massive
overhaul after the Revolution. Prior to 1952, fewer
than 50 percent of all primary-age children
attended school. Today, 80 percent of the age
group are enrolled in primary school, and 68
percent attend secondary school.

The Revolution dramatically expanded
educational opportunities. Free education became
available to all. Government spending on
education increased and as a result so did the

number of primary schools. But this rapid increase came at the expense of quality. A growing population put enormous strain on resources and resulted in overcrowded classrooms and schools in bad condition. With a very large student-to-teacher ratio, parents began to resort to private lessons for their children to supplement their learning. The decline in the standard of public schools created a space for private education.

Today the Egyptian middle and upper classes choose to send their children to private schools. The best of these are foreign-language schools where the teaching is in English or French, and Arabic is merely a second language. (Children can spend their entire lives in Egypt and yet have poor Arabic.) Graduating from these schools helps facilitate entrance to foreign universities, both in Egypt and abroad.

School is compulsory for the first nine years. In practice, however, poorer families, particularly in rural areas, often remove their children from school and send them to work at a young age. The government does not strictly enforce attendance.

Apart from the old-established Egyptian universities, which teach all subjects in Arabic, there has been a recent boom in private Egyptian and foreign universities (sometimes affiliated with universities abroad). The oldest and most prestigious private university is the American University in Egypt, whose alumni include Queen Rania of Jordan.

National Service

Military service is compulsory for males between the ages of eighteen and thirty-five. They must have other male siblings (an only son is exempt) and be physically and mentally fit. Those in full-time education are excused until they finish their studies. The length of military service ranges from one year for those with university education to three years for those without. Before the 1952 Revolution conscription could be avoided if one paid the government a sum of money, but afterward this option was abolished.

National service is a miserable and demoralizing experience for most young men, who suffer from repeated bullying in the name of discipline but who have to serve before they can get a permit to work or travel abroad.

There are, of course, those who go on to have a career in the army. For young men with an education, the army is one way of guaranteeing a government job that pays relatively well, provides benefits, and grants power and social status. For those with no education, the army can be their only chance of a paid job.

FAMILY OCCASIONS

Family occasions are important events in Egypt. They are colorful affairs soaked in tradition and rituals, where the help and participation of family members is considered an obligation.

Births

In the cities, women generally give birth in hospitals attended by a doctor. In rural areas, women are more likely to give birth at home assisted by a midwife and in the company of female family members.

Approximately a week after the birth a party, called the *subu'*, is given for the baby, and friends and acquaintances bring their gifts. A customary gift for this occasion is gold jewelry, regardless of the baby's gender. Babies can accumulate a large amount of jewelry at birth, which is generally put away as an investment for its future. To celebrate the birth, children are given sweets and gifts, and adults receive sugared almonds. Special songs are sung, women ululate, and the newborn is dressed in a special white gown.

In Egypt all boys, Christian as well as Muslim, are circumcised, usually a few days after birth. Traditionally there was a party for this event, particularly in rural areas; but today this is less common, as boys are generally circumcised in a hospital or clinic.

Lineage is important and is made official by the registration of a newborn's name. An Egyptian's full name, in theory, is never-ending. A baby is given a name, which is followed by the father's first name, then the grandfather's first name, then the great-grandfather's, and so on. Finally comes the surname. In official documents and for proof of identity Egyptians use three or four of these names. Socially, the first name and the surname are used. Thus, if a Mohamed Badawi has a son called Ahmed, his name is Ahmed Mohamed Badawi. If Ahmed's wife gives birth to a baby girl and calls her Layla, her name is Layla Ahmed Mohamed Badawi. Socially, people will call her Layla Badawi.

Marriage

Marriage is the most important rite of passage and celebration in an Egyptian's life. For most men, marriage is the transition to adulthood. And for women, it is the beginning of the road to motherhood. In a society where the family is so important, the young are eager to start their own.

Romantic relationships are difficult to sustain. It is rare for unmarried couples to meet without a chaperone and arranged marriages are common. This often means an introduction by the families. Bridal consent for the marriage is very important and required by religion, and rarely will anyone be forced into marriage. If a couple develops a relationship outside the family setting, family approval for the union is essential. A marriage in Egypt is seen not only as a marriage of individuals but a marriage of families. In-laws interact with each other frequently.

In most families, weddings are a time of joy, with much pomp and ceremony surrounding the event. But with all the happiness that comes with it, it also brings a huge financial burden. Parents of the bride and groom, who bear the cost of the wedding, start saving up for the occasion soon after a child is born.

The process begins when the family of the groom makes an appointment with the prospective bride's family to ask for her hand in marriage. The groom must reveal his income and state the amount of dowry (*muqaddam*) he is prepared to pay; a groom must pay the dowry before the consummation of the marriage. If the bride's family accepts, they seal the bond by reading a specific verse of the Qur'an called the *fatha*. The parents then set a date for the engagement, which is usually a small party at the bride's house. During the engagement, rings are worn on the right hand and are switched to the left hand on the day of the wedding.

The engagement period allows the couple freedom to go out unchaperoned. It is also the time to get their new home ready. The groom's family traditionally provides the house, while the bride's family is responsible for furnishing it. It is common for couples who cannot afford a new home to move in with the groom's family.

Henna Night
When a woman is to be married, a celebration is held for her called *leilet el henna* (night of the henna). Her female relatives and friends gather to sing, dance, and perform a set of rituals to bless her approaching marriage. Her hands are dotted with henna paste, a tradition dating back to the time when henna was used cosmetically.

The Wedding
Egyptian wedding parties are grand celebrations with food and music and entertainment. The groom's family traditionally pays for the wedding ceremony.

Today, especially for the upper classes, wedding parties have become such lavish affairs that families may choose to split the cost.

The *zaffa*, the procession, is an adrenalin-pumped event. The couple is surrounded by guests and the air fills with the sounds of trumpets blowing and drums beating. Women break into piercing ululations to let everyone know that a wedding is taking place. While the procession is open to all, the reception is for invited guests only. In some rural areas the couple's furniture is paraded through the town on its way to its new home.

Marriage in Egypt is a civil contract and is usually performed by an official. Religious ceremonies are part of the process but cannot replace the civil element. Women keep their family name after marriage.

Death

Egyptians are a religious people. Death is considered the will of God. In Egypt, as in many Arab cultures, grief is expressed openly.

Islamic tradition dictates that burial take place within twenty-four hours of death, except in extraordinary circumstances.

On the day of the funeral and after the sunset prayers, people wishing to pay their respects attend a mosque where the family of the deceased has arranged a Qur'an reading. As the sheikh reads verses of the Qur'an, mourners pay their respects to the bereaved. The sheikh will take a break every half hour; one should wait for one of these to make one's departure. Plain Turkish coffee is served at these occasions. Formal dress and dark ties for men are expected. Meanwhile, the house of the deceased is prepared to receive female mourners. Visitors should dress in black as a sign of respect.

A three-day mourning period follows the burial. Relatives wear black during this time and a wife who has lost her husband wears black for a year. Family and close friends attend to the needs of the deceased's immediate family; they may even move in for the mourning period.

Seven days after the death, there is a reading of the Qur'an. Family and close friends gather at the house of the deceased, where each one will read a section. Forty days after the death, another service takes place at the house.

In Egypt flowers are not sent at funerals. They are reserved for celebrations. Sending flowers to a funeral would be an immense *faux pas* as it would imply that the funeral is a happy occasion.

DAILY LIFE
In the Town
Internal migration has put huge pressure on Egypt's towns and cities and resulted in extreme overcrowding. Town planning is very weak.

The routine of urban life is not so different from in the West. People commute to work, and socialize on weekends and holidays. While economic pressures, overcrowding, traffic congestion, and pollution can make daily life a grind, social life generally helps to alleviate the stress.

Because Egyptian women are enthusiastic cooks who prefer to start from the basics, they like to buy fresh fruit and vegetables from the grocer, meat from the butcher, and fish from the fishmonger. Supermarket produce is

seen as inferior and is generally more expensive.

Urban Networking

Urban households also have a small network of people outside the family who provide essential services. The *bawwab* (doorman), the *baqqal* (grocer), and the *makwagi* (ironing person) are a very important trio in an Egyptian's life.

The **bawwab**'s official job is to act as a security guard, but he can also be a caretaker, a runner of errands, and the person who washes your car. He lives in a small room in the building and gets a modest salary from the residents.

In Egypt most **baqqaleen** (plural of *baqqal*) deliver groceries to your door. Daily needs like bread, milk, butter, canned goods, and bottled water are just a phone call away. Once a relationship has been developed with the local *baqqal*, one can use a credit system and pay at the end of the month.

Most areas have a local **makwagi**. Send your clothes in a bag and they will be returned pressed and folded or on hangers.

In the Country

Rural life is more traditional. Family structure within the home is more rigid, with men

exercising unquestionable authority. Fewer women work outside the home. The pace of life is rhythmic. Farmers wake at dawn and go to their local mosque to pray together. They spend the day working in the fields, breaking for noon prayers. They come home for a meal and a sleep, and may go back to the fields later. They return home for a light evening meal with the family.

Ambitions in the rural areas used to be simple: people wanted a home, a family, and land to cultivate. As the children grew up, they helped on the land, so they were considered an investment and a form of social security for the parents.

Nasser's Revolution changed the dynamics. Farming was regulated, and land taken away from the big landowners and redistributed among the peasantry, who were given land titles. Deeds were inherited, which meant that land was divided between children and then grandchildren. Population growth resulted in scarcity of land and families no longer had enough crops to trade but just enough to sustain themselves.

Today, in the countryside, education rather than manual labor is seen as securing a child's future. The cost of education and upbringing places a financial burden on parents, who are now choosing to have fewer children.

Fashion

Up until the 1970s, most urban Egyptian women wore European dress, which was a statement of modernity and secularism, and was in sharp contrast to rural clothes, which consisted of a long, loose dress and a head scarf.

Upper-class urban Egyptian women still sport Western clothes, but a recent Islamist trend has meant that the majority of Egyptian women today cover their heads. You can see a range of styles, from the traditional long, loose robe (*gallabiyya*) and *higab* (head scarf), to jeans and fashionable tops with creative head coverings.

TIME OUT

Egyptians, who enjoy their weekend on a Friday, love to socialize outdoors, taking walks, boat trips, or having picnics. But the hot weather and financial restraints mean that most socializing takes place indoors, generally in people's homes.

Those who can afford to eat out usually do so in groups. Tables for six are much more common than tables for two. Watching life go by is a favorite pastime, as families and groups of friends congregate in the outdoor spaces to enjoy drinks and water pipes or play a game of backgammon.

THE NILE

Put away images of a sleepy river with a single sailboat gliding romantically through empty waters. The Nile is the Egyptian playground. It is a hub of activity, toward which Egyptians gravitate for many of their social activities.

Party boats zip up and down, blaring loud Arabic music to the cheers and claps of the passengers. Large lunch and dinner cruise boats crawl along, hiding from view the belly dancer and the lavish buffets inside. And if you want to join the well-to-do parading their yachts on the Nile, you can rent your own.

Still available on the Nile are romantic *felucca* trips; a sunset on this type of traditional sailboat is magical. A *felucca* can be rented in half-hour slots, is usually crewed by professionals, and you can bring your own food and music.

The banks of the Nile are also home to much activity. They are flanked by restaurants and bars where the well-heeled go to dine and dance. Brides and grooms have their picture taken by the Nile, accompanied by  large numbers of relatives. Fishermen set up tables and chairs and linger for hours waiting for a catch. Young couples, who have few places to go to in public, line the banks with their backs to society's prying eyes.

Vendors have astutely made a living from all the hubbub. So much is sold on the street: from balloons for the children to corn on the cob and grilled sweet potato. Cold drinks, hot drinks, toys, and fake Rolex watches can all be bought al fresco.

SHOPPING FOR PLEASURE

In Egypt there is a great array of places to shop in, from upmarket boutiques to open-air bazaars.

American-style malls have seen a surge in popularity in recent years. The main cities all have malls with multiplex cinemas, shops, and cafés. Young people treat them like community clubs: they meet there, window-shop, sip fruit juice, and mingle in the comfort of the air-conditioning.

Egyptians prefer to buy their spices, clothes,

jewelry, and household goods in open-air markets. These are generally open from 10:00 a.m. and close at around 8:00 p.m. All shops close during the Friday prayer.

In most bazaars shopkeepers will try to lure you into their shops with promises of bargains and discounts. Some have been known to trap naïve travelers into buying with sensational claims. If someone trying to sell you incense tells you it is the same one that Cleopatra used, it probably isn't . . .

In modern supermarkets and malls haggling is not done; it is very much part of the process at bazaars and open-air markets. Experienced shoppers will tell you that there are certain tricks to getting a good bargain. First, don't waste your and the seller's time haggling over something that costs very little. Don't haggle unless you intend to buy. Striking a deal is a verbal contract and it is considered rude to come to an agreement over a price and then walk away without buying, especially if you have spent some time bringing the price down.

BARGAINING TECHNIQUE

There are several techniques to haggling: this is just one. If you see something you like, inquire about something else first. Being too eager sends the price up automatically. Eventually, turn the shopkeeper's attention to the item you originally wanted. Find out about the price. Say you will check elsewhere and be back. Do the same at several shops. When you have a reasonable idea of what it costs generally, you may then go back to one of the shops and begin the real bargaining.

Don't look excited about an item: rather, try to find fault with it. The seller knows this is part of the game. When he feels you are truly interested in buying, he may offer you tea and make conversation. Once you've agreed on a price that you feel comfortable with, shake hands and pay.

It is better to pay in cash for items sold at bazaars as all shops have to pay commission for credit cards and will therefore charge you more.

Beware of tour guides who insist on taking you to a specific shop for items that are sold in many places. They may be getting a commission, something that is sure to push up prices.

CULTURAL ACTIVITIES
Cinema

Egypt has had a strong cinematic tradition since the 1930s. Movies produced there are watched across the Arab world. The golden age of Egyptian cinema was in the 1940s and 1950s, from which emerged one of Egypt's best cinematic exports— Omar Sharif. Today, the industry has lost a bit of its shimmer. Many film critics think that the quality of Egyptian cinema has declined since the 1970s, with poorly developed scripts and recycled ideas. While in the last ten years there has been a cinema revival spearheaded by young filmmakers, it has yet to really take off.

There is a wide range of movie theaters. At the top end are the multiplexes, mainly in the big cities. The middle-range cinemas are grand buildings built in the 1940s and 1950s, with high ceilings and balconies, but sadly these are run-down. Up-to-date Hollywood films are screened at the top and middle-range cinemas and are subtitled in Arabic. Below this level are the cheapest cinemas, where you can watch several movies with one ticket. These show old Indian, martial arts, and Arabic films, and action movies.

The Egyptian cinema experience is peppered with audience action. People will talk throughout the film—about the film, about daily business, about anything that comes to mind, really. Babies may cry, cell phones may ring, and none of this generally bothers other moviegoers. Egyptians are expressive and emotive, even in movie theaters. The lower down the movie theater chain you go, the more interactive the audience becomes. They may shout at the screen in disapproval or scream out plot suggestions to the actors. It is all part of the experience.

As the film plays, don't be surprised if the lights are switched on mid-sentence and the movie is paused. This is the unavoidable break that allows people to visit the restroom and satisfy their nicotine cravings. Moreover, the credits at the end seem to be of no interest to most patrons and, once the plot twist has been resolved near the finish, many will get up and start leaving.

All movies must pass Egypt's censor: scenes involving sex, extreme violence, or anything considered blasphemous will be cut out.

Theater

The theater scene is not as vibrant as it once was. In its heyday, Egyptian theater consisted of colorful puppetry and oral folk literature in which professional storytellers recounted popular tales. After the Revolution theater was encouraged: production was state funded, original screenplays were written, and Western scripts were translated into Arabic. Today commercial theater caters mainly to the tastes of Arab tourists from the Gulf States, who flock to Egypt in the summer in search of slapstick humor. Ticket prices are expensive for most Egyptians.

Music

Egyptian music, like most Middle Eastern music, is rhythmic and emotional. A steady percussion rhythm is overlaid with poetic instrumental or vocal melodies.

Instruments used in traditional Arabic music include stringed instruments like the *'ud*, a pear-shaped, short-necked string instrument that resembles a lute, and the *kamanga*, a violin. Wind instruments like the *nay* and the *mizmar*, two different types of flute, also feature. As for percussion, there is a variety of drums, tambourines, and cymbals.

Performers expect feedback from their audiences. In Egypt, a silent audience is a disapproving one. Audience members will generally hum, clap, sing along, cheer, or cry to music. Song requests will be made, repeat performances called for, and appreciation shouted out at the climactic moments in the performance.

Modern Egyptian music resembles Western pop music, with synthesizers and computers at its heart. Egyptians are proud of local Amr Diab, who took Egyptian music beyond the borders to perform with Rai superstar Khaled and Greek singing diva Angela Dimitrou. In 1998, Diab won the Worldwide Music Award in Monaco.

Belly Dancing

Belly dancing is the Western name for *Ra's Baladi* ("local dancing"), the sexy Middle Eastern dance, which some historians believe was once a fertility ritual. The dance consists of circular hip and arm movements that mimic the emotions and rhythm of the music.

Egyptians have a very conflicted relationship with belly dancing. On the one hand, they consider it a national art and many families hire belly dancers to entertain at wedding parties. Men, women, and children cheer on the belly dancer at such gatherings and encourage young girls to go and join her on the dance floor.

At the same time, belly dancers are considered loose and their world sleazy. "Nice girls" don't grow up wanting to be belly dancers!

EATING OUT

Egyptian cuisine is often accused by other Arabs of being poor; this is mainly because the good dishes are difficult to create and take a lot of preparation, so are more suited to domestic than restaurant cooking. Egyptians therefore prefer to eat at home. They are accustomed to being fed by a mother or a wife and don't see the point of going out to eat when a perfectly good meal can be enjoyed without leaving the house.

Because good Egyptian cuisine is confined to the home, it is isolated, so in different houses one can find a lot of variation on a single dish. There are a few restaurants that serve Egyptian food, but the quality does not compare to home cooking.

Egyptian cuisine has many influences: Turkish, Middle Eastern, as well as roots dating back to the time of the Ancient Egyptians. While, in Europe, food is considered part of the cultural heritage, unfortunately in Egypt there has been no move to preserve cooking techniques and recipes. Given this, an outsider is likely to taste only a minute amount of genuine Egyptian cuisine.

Eating establishments range from street stalls serving up local food to exclusive restaurants offering international cuisine, but good restaurants with creative menus are scarce and are found mainly in hotels. They are also expensive, which means that the majority of Egyptians eat out mainly when they're in a hurry.

Throughout Egypt, fixed stalls or little shops serve Egyptian fast food. Many look uninviting, but don't be put off by first impressions: they are often clean and quick. Street carts, however, are not a hygienic option, as the food stays out in the sun too long, and attracts flies.

Most mid-range sit-down restaurants serve a bland "continental" menu with unadventurous pastas, meats, and salads. Egyptians are a meat-loving people, so vegetarians may get bored with the unexciting options around. The larger cities also have the well-known fast-food chains.

Egyptian cuisine is not typically spicy but Egyptians cook with huge amounts of ghee (clarified butter), so beware of heartburn.

The main staple is bread, which is eaten with everything. The most common, *'aish baladi*, is like pita but made with coarse wholewheat flour.

Ful and *Ta'miya*

Along with bread, the indigenous fava bean, known locally as *ful*, supplies most Egyptians with their daily calorific intake. It can be cooked in several ways and everyone has their favorite. It can be cooked with ghee or olive oil; topped with tahini or chopped tomatoes; sprinkled with cumin, or complemented with lemon. It can be served in pockets of *baladi* bread or served on a platter. Egyptians will eat *ful* for breakfast, lunch, or dinner. It is nutritious and filling.

Ful beans are also used to make the popular *ta'miya*, or falafel, as it is known in other parts of the world. The beans are mashed, spiced, and then fried (to the east of the Mediterranean, falafel are made with chickpeas rather than *ful*).

Koshari

Koshari, another Egyptian favorite, is a dish made up of rice, noodles, lentils, tomato sauce, and fried onions. It is served in hole-in-the-wall shops distinguishable by their huge piles of rice and noodles in the window. Ordering at one of these places is easy: you just shout out the number of portions you want. A little vinegar with garlic can be added for more oomph.

Molokhiyya

Molokhiyya, distinctively Egyptian, is a leafy, green, summer vegetable. Cooked in chicken broth to make a thick soup, it can be served over rice with chicken or rabbit on the side, or on its own. *Molokhiyya* is hardly ever found in restaurants; and a domestic cook's talent is often measured by how good their *molokhiyya* is.

Meat

For the great majority of Egyptians meat is a luxury, and in most homes it is used in small quantities and served with vegetables or rice. Restaurants, however, specialize in meat dishes, especially grills.

A *kababgi* is a restaurant that serves Egyptian-style kebabs and other grills. A typical platter consists of *kabab*, *kofta* (minced lamb flavored with onions and spices), and lamb cutlets. When ordering, it is customary to order by the kilo (half a kilo is usually enough for two people). Also on offer are grilled chicken and Egypt's national delicacy, pigeons stuffed with seasoned rice.

Fish

Fish is eaten everywhere. In the rural areas it is mainly river fish, which is considered inferior to saltwater fish from the Mediterranean. Some fish also comes from the Red Sea. Fish restaurants serve a straightforward barbecued grill or fish deep-fried in batter. You can pick the fish yourself at the restaurant tank.

Fruits and Vegetables

Egypt's very wide range of local fruits and vegetables are generally eaten in season, as imports are too expensive for most people. If one's pocket allows, imported fruits and vegetables can be bought year-round at the upmarket supermarkets.

Vegetable stalls sell Egyptian fresh fruit and vegetables. Because Egyptians buy for families, fruit vendors find it curious when foreigners come in and ask for just one apple!

Desserts

Popular desserts include rice pudding, similar to that in the West but infused with rose water. *Mahalabiya* is a white semolina-based pudding garnished with pistachios. *Om 'Ali* is a bread pudding made with filo pastry, milk, nuts, and spices. Also very common are oriental sweets such as baklava.

TABLE MANNERS

Most dining establishments in Egypt allow smoking and it is difficult to find a nonsmoking restaurant. It would be rude to tell an Egyptian to put out his or her cigarette.

Bread is eaten with every meal and, if eating a stew or a dip, it is normal to use pita bread in place of cutlery. Starters and dips are often eaten communally: everyone dips their bread into the same plate. Don't worry: knives and forks will be on the table at all restaurants.

As we have seen, if invited for a meal out, it is polite to insist on paying. This can end up in a long back and forth between the leaders of the party. The person with the strongest will usually pays. It is courteous to return the invitation.

THE *AHWA*

The *ahwa*, the traditional Egyptian coffee shop, is the social hub of every Egyptian male. It is where men meet, talk, and unwind, where politics and society are discussed, theories formulated, and rumors spread. Men go there after work to pour the day's tension into a game of backgammon, and let the stress fade with the smoke of their *shisha* (water pipe). Smoking *shisha* is more than just a nicotine fix; it is a social affair that should not be hurried.

Each neighborhood is dotted with *ahawi* (plural of *ahwa*), some more rustic than others, some more polished, but all pretty basic as far as interiors go. An *ahwa*, particularly in residential areas, has a loyal clientele. It consists of an indoor section with tables and chairs that overflow onto the pavement. The menu is limited: there is tea, coffee, and a variety of other hot or cold drinks. While women are not actually banned from entering, a traditional *ahwa* is definitely a man's place. There are several *ahawi* that welcome women but these are mainly aimed at tourists.

DRINKING

Tea

Egyptians are avid tea drinkers. Dried tea leaves are boiled in water over a stove, which makes the cup a lot stronger than tea bags. Egyptians drink their tea sweet: if ordering tea in an *ahwa*, it will usually be served with sugar, a lot of it. If you don't want sugar, ask for it with none. Otherwise don't stir. A refreshing drink is mint tea, where a sprig or two of fresh mint is added to the tea.

Tea is usually served in glasses. Tea with milk is generally a breakfast drink and will be made with boiled milk rather than boiled water.

Coffee

Traditionally the coffee drunk in Egypt is "Turkish coffee," though there has recently been an

explosion of fashionable European-style cafés that
serve capuccinos and lattes.

The traditional cup is thick and strong. It is
made from finely ground coffee beans, infused
with cardamom and brewed in a small pot. The
coffee is not filtered, so, when served in little cups,
the grains sink to the bottom. Because the sugar is
mixed in with the coffee prior to brewing, you
should specify when ordering how sweet
you want it. *Ahwa sada* means coffee
with no sugar, *ahwa 'ariha* contains
little sugar, *ahwa mazbuta* has a little
more sugar, and *ahwa ziada* is sweet.

Other Hot Drinks

Egyptians enjoy herbal tea, the drink of choice
when they have consumed all the caffeine they
can for a day. It is also said to have medicinal
properties. Popular teas are hibiscus, aniseed,
cinnamon, and caraway.

Sahlab is a milky drink made from orchid
bulbs and served with nuts and cinnamon. In the
winter, Egyptians love *hommos el sham*, a thin
soup of chickpea and chili that is treated as a hot
drink and served in a glass.

Cold Drinks

Fruit juice stands are one of Egypt's real delights.
Particularly in the summer, people bunch around

shops and stands that blend fresh juices and juice cocktails. The most popular is sugarcane juice, a great pick-me-up, especially in the summer heat. Also on offer are mouthwatering combinations of strawberry, mango, banana, and orange. Sugar is always added for the Egyptian sweet tooth, so if you don't want sugar, just ask.

Other cold drinks include licorice-based *'Er soos* and *Tamr Hindi*, made from tamarind.

Alcohol

Drinking alcohol is prohibited by Islam, but in practice some Muslims do drink. The many Christians in Egypt are free to drink alcohol.

About a decade ago, the local beer was flat, the wine vinegary, and the whiskey lethal! Thankfully this is not the case today. Egypt has a booming wine industry. Beer is also produced locally: Stella, a light lager, is the most popular.

Alcohol can be bought from liquor stores in the cities, from hotels, and from some bars and restaurants. Imported beer, wine, and spirits are available but expensive. They are usually found in hotels and upmarket restaurants and bars.

Buza is an alcoholic drink traditionally made from fermented bread. It is homemade, has little alcohol content, and is found in rural Egypt. Once popular but now disappearing, it is a refreshing drink in the summer, if you can find it.

BARS AND NIGHTCLUBS

Egyptian nightlife is as multifaceted as its society. From the seedy bars of Cairo's Pyramids Road with their belly dancers and Arabic music to the swanky, shiny nightclubs of Sharm el Sheikh, Egypt has it all.

In Cairo and Alexandria, old bars that once catered mainly to the expatriate community now play host to the country's intellectuals and artists. They are a bit rough around the edges but have a nostalgic feel, lacking in the smarter places.

TIPPING

In Egypt, wages are much lower than in the West and many people depend on tips (*ba'shish*). Wealthy Egyptians tip their way through most things. A tip is not seen as a reward for exceptional service, but as a regular small supplement. Someone who carries your bags expects a tip, as does the parking attendant who helps you park your car, and the usher who shows you to your seat at a cinema. For *ba'shish*, your butcher will get you better meat from the back of the shop, and your doorman will run errands for you.

When an Egyptian refers to a "cabaret," he is probably referring to a nightclub that has dinner, drinks, and a belly dance show. Traditional Egyptians consider these places to be little more than institutionalized brothels.

It is sometimes difficult to remember that Egypt is a conservative society when you step into the voguish bars and nightclubs that dot the large cities. Hidden from society's restrictive rules, the wealthy and the Westernized drink and party the night away behind closed doors.

SPORTS

In Egypt, sport is synonymous with football. Egyptians are football crazy and take it incredibly seriously. The two main Cairo teams, Ahly and Zamalek, attract the greatest support across the country. Rivalry between them is fierce.

Egypt is the reigning African football champion, having won the African Cup of Nations in 2006. Football fever swept the country as men, women, boys, and girls celebrated on the streets wearing Egypt's colors: black, white, and red.

Many streets are turned into football fields in the summer, regardless of traffic. Every city has its own social club (the bigger cities have several), where children go to train in their chosen sports. It is also a meeting place for families and many will have their Friday lunches at the clubs.

Egyptians have excelled at a few sports on an international championship level, mainly handball and squash. This has turned the nation's attention a little to these sports and people may follow them on television or live at big matches.

A newcomer on the Egyptian sporting scene is golf. Golf courses have been multiplying over the last few years, with Egypt boasting some of the region's best. Savvy tour operators have designed package holidays specifically for the avid golfer.

OUT OF TOWN
On national holidays, religious feasts, and sometimes weekends, Egyptians head to the coast. Day trips to Alexandria and the Mediterranean beaches are popular destinations for  family trips. Those who can afford it have second homes on the north coast or Sinai and spend their summer weekends away from the frenzy of the city.

chapter seven

TRAVEL, HEALTH, & SAFETY

Egypt is a traveler's treasure trove, with renowned archaeological sights, beaches, and deserts. But it is overcrowded and polluted. Most tourists are shielded by organized tours, taken from sight to restaurant without having to brave the Egyptians' Egypt. If traveling independently, however, it is important to be aware of road etiquette and health and safety hazards.

ROADS AND TRAFFIC

A bird's-eye view of one of Egypt's main squares would look like an Escher drawing: crowded and busy, with no one quite sure where things begin and where they end. To a foreign visitor, it is chaotic. But Egyptians know there is a system within this chaos. Pedestrians, carts, and animals weave through cars in a calculated tango. There exists a sort of Driving Darwinism, a survival of the fittest wherein timid drivers will not get very far. And while there is tension on the streets, this rarely turns into aggression. Most of the time, the stress is diffused by a little humor and patience.

Driving

Driving in Egypt is stressful, but foreigners often remark that being a passenger is far scarier than being a driver; at least, when driving, you exercise a degree of control.

Egyptian drivers are impatient. Western rules concerning "right of way," signaling, and use of mirrors do not apply. Lanes are disregarded, with sometimes as many as four cars side by side in a two-lane street. Side view mirrors are folded in to save space. Cars cut in front of one another regularly and everyone always  seems to be in a rush. And then there is the use of the horn. A foreigner has trouble deciphering its meaning: sometimes it means "hurry up," sometimes "be careful," and sometimes it is used to greet other drivers. Drivers who flash their headlights are warning you to stay out of their way. Traffic lights are frequently ignored. More often than not, a traffic policeman will be present at main junctions to direct traffic. So what does a newcomer do when faced with such challenges? The golden rule is: look ahead, worry about what's in front of you, not what's behind you, and don't be intimidated by other drivers beeping at you. If you can't beat them, join them!

Despite attempts at improvement, many areas still have inadequate roads with bad paving, potholes, and poor signage. Intercity roads are generally in good condition. Rural mud roads, often unmarked, can challenge the best of drivers.

Speed limits are taken seriously, especially on intercity roads. Traffic police operate handheld radar equipment to pick up speeding drivers. If caught speeding, you will have your license confiscated. You will then have to go to traffic headquarters to pay a fine and retrieve it, a long and bureaucratic process.

On the road, drivers have an "us vs. them" attitude toward the police. They show solidarity by flashing their headlights at oncoming traffic to warn it to slow down if radar is in operation.

For offenses such as talking on your cell phone while driving, not having your seat belt on, or parking where forbidden, you may have your license confiscated. In these cases many Egyptians pay the traffic policeman to "forget" the incident. However, never under any circumstance will an *officer* accept such a bribe, so don't offer money to anyone who has stars on their lapels!

An international driver's license is valid for one year. Foreigners can also use their home licenses for up to three months. Residents can apply for an Egyptian license. Make sure you always have ID papers, driver's license, and registration papers on you as there are regular checkpoints where you will be asked to produce this documentation.

Parking

Parking meters are only now being piloted in a few areas. You can park in most places except in front of government buildings, embassies, and the residences of diplomats and politicians. Signs are not always very clear. Usually the best approach is: if another car is parked there, you can park too.

The upside is that parking on the streets is free. The downside is the difficulty of finding a parking space. Egyptians have mastered the art of parallel parking, squeezing into the most unlikely gaps. In the cities, and particularly in Cairo, a degree of creativity has to be used. Although double-parking is illegal, it is very common and rarely attracts police attention. If you are double-parking, do not set your emergency brake and keep your wheels aligned. A driver whose car you have blocked will push your car out of the way. So do not be shocked when you come out to find your car slightly shifted from its original spot, or a random stranger pushing it. He is probably not trying to steal it.

In most central areas, a parking attendant, called a *menadi*, is there to find you a parking spot and help you fit into it, for a small fee. Sometimes, people give their keys to the *menadi*, who will find a parking spot for them. Not every *menadi* is an employee of the state, some wear badges, some are hired by restaurants or popular establishments for their clientele, and some work freelance, but all are treated equally by Egyptians regardless of whether or not they are "official."

Accidents

An accident has to be reported at a police station if a driver wants to file an insurance claim. The number of people covered by insurance is low. Uninsured drivers who have crashed into each other prefer to settle the dispute on the spot without resorting to the system, providing there are no injuries and no serious damage. Status and wealth play a part here. If there is serious damage and the person at fault is richer (drives a better car), he or she will probably pay for it. Settlement really depends on the drivers. Very often, if there is no serious damage, people will get out of their cars, make a little fuss, and then go their own way.

Pedestrians

Drivers are not the only ones who need to display a little feistiness; pedestrians must also show a fair share. Smooth sidewalks are practically nonexistent. Walking in Egypt, particularly in Cairo, is like being on a mini assault course. Sidewalks are rudely interrupted by litter, parked cars, holes, pipes, and electrical wires.

Crossing a busy street poses one of the most difficult challenges and newcomers have been known to take a cab across a square rather than face it. Pedestrian crossings are ignored by traffic. Black-and-white stripes across a street do not, in practice, mean right of way for pedestrians.

Assertion and even aggression are required. Waiting for cars to slow down can leave you by the side of the road indefinitely. You need to be focused. Take that first step and cross. Stop in the middle of the road if you feel a car is coming too fast; let it pass and move to the next lane. If you hesitate and go back and forth, you are likely to be knocked over. If it all gets too much, find a group of Egyptians and cross with them. Eventually, you will know how to walk the walk.

LOCAL TRANSPORTATION

Public transportation is used mainly by the working class and students. The wealthy rarely use it, except perhaps when traveling between cities. Egyptians are curious about foreigners and on a journey will use the opportunity to strike up a conversation and ask about the world beyond their borders. If spoken to, it is polite to answer. If an interesting conversation is struck up, you may even be invited for a glass of tea.

The Metro and Trams

Cairo's underground train system, the Metro, is the fastest and cheapest way to travel. The lines run only through the heart of the city; more are being planned. The metro is clean and efficient. The first car is reserved for women only, although women are free to use all the cars.

Cairo and Alexandria both have tram networks. In Cairo, the system is limited to the northwestern Heliopolis district. In Alexandria, the network is extensive and the system reliable.

Buses and Minibuses

Riding a bus can be a perilous affair. Buses are old, rusty, and severely overcrowded in the rush hour, and hardly ever come to a complete halt, except in a traffic jam. People chase the moving buses in an attempt to get on and those who don't make it may end up hanging off the doors. The lucky ones pack themselves in, leaving hardly any room to maneuver. (Pickpocketing is a risk.) Remarkably, the bus conductor manages to zigzag his way through to sell tickets.

There are also air-conditioned minibus services across the main cities. They are slightly more expensive than normal buses but less crowded. Standing is not allowed and a minibus will start moving as soon as all the seats have been filled.

Microbuses

While microbuses, seating about twelve people, have fixed routes and fixed fares, it is not easy to find out what these are. Usually someone at the door calls out the destination; this is also the person who collects the money. If there is no one on the door, then it is customary to pass the fare forward, where the person in the front seat becomes the designated conductor. You can get on and off where you want. Simply hail one anywhere along the route and get on.

Microbus drivers are infamous for their reckless driving, so do not expect a smooth ride.

Taxis

This is the most convenient way to travel. There are plenty of taxis and fares are cheap. Taxis can be hailed anywhere on the street. In Cairo, they are painted black and white, in Alexandria orange and black. Other cities have other color codes.

The high rate of unemployment has meant that many educated men resort to working as cab drivers. Some have rudimentary English, enough to give prices and understand simple directions. Others, particularly those in the tourist areas, will surprise you with their command of the language.

Cab drivers love to chat, especially with foreigners. It is common for a cab driver to act as an unofficial tour guide, pointing out important buildings and monuments. Politics is their

favorite topic: they often expect Western passengers to explain their countries' foreign policies vis-à-vis the Middle East, skillfully putting the passenger on the defensive. It is up to you how far to engage in such conversations.

Especially during rush hours, it is normal for a cab to take on other passengers. If you are in a hurry, you can ask not to have other passengers on board or to be dropped off first.

Women should always try to sit in the back of the cab, especially if they are alone. It would be uncomfortable for the driver to have a strange woman sitting close to him in the front.

Although cabs are required by law to operate their meters, these are usually old and do not show the current prices. No one in Egypt goes by the meter. Locals generally know what to pay. Inquire at your hotel or ask a friend how much you should pay. In general foreigners are expected to pay more than locals. When you hail a cab, shout out your destination. Do not haggle over the price before getting in. If the suggested price is too high, get another cab.

Many cabs are in bad condition. Doors may not close properly, seats may have worn out padding, and some windows may not open or close. Despite this, drivers who own their own vehicles consider their car their little space in the world and put great effort into personalizing it. Family photos on the dashboard and religious symbols hanging from the mirror are typical, or even stuffed toys and mini-chandeliers.

Most cab drivers have cell phones. You can establish a relationship and arrange to be dropped off at, and picked up from, appointments.

Yellow Taxis

In 2006, two companies set up cab services with air-conditioned taxis resembling New York's famous yellow cabs. Unlike the old black-and-white cabs, the new taxis do use their meters and, while they are more expensive, they are more comfortable. These cabs can be hailed on the street or they can be ordered by phone.

INTERCITY TRAVEL

There are many options for intercity travel in Egypt, suitable for both the budget and the luxury traveler. Tourist police may stop foreigners and ask where they are from and where they are headed. Do not be alarmed—tourists' safety is their responsibility and it is standard procedure.

Planes

Egypt Air and a variety of charter airlines operate routes between cities. A passport is not required for travel inside Egypt—usually any form of ID with a picture will be sufficient (though a passport will be needed at a hotel). On internal flights, there are different prices for Egyptians and for foreigners. Resident foreigners pay Egyptian rates but must produce their residence visa when purchasing a ticket.

Internal flights rarely run on time and are often overbooked. Expect delays.

Buses

A variety of bus companies connects cities and towns in Egypt. Tickets can be bought at the bus station and sometimes on the bus.

"Deluxe air-conditioned buses" in no way guarantee luxury travel (even if the brochure promises that). At best, you will have a

designated seat, relatively clean toilets on board, and snacks. Sleeping can prove difficult as the onboard entertainment tends to be a loud Egyptian film on a screen at the front of the bus.

On non–air-conditioned buses, the experience is different. While seats may be designated, packs of people traveling together, sometimes whole families, will want to sit together. There will be a lot of commotion on the trip, with people and their belongings taking up space and air.

Trains

Like most things in Egypt, trains are defined by price and type of traveler. The more direct trains cost more and are mainly used by tourists and affluent Egyptians. They have comfortable, air-conditioned, first-class carriages. Second class is also comfortable, but not always air-conditioned. In third class the seats are not padded, and the carriages can be overcrowded and uncomfortable on long journeys. Sleepers are available to places like Luxor and Aswan in the south of Egypt.

ACCOMMODATION

Hotels

Egypt has accommodation types to suit every budget. Prices are rarely negotiable—never in the top- and middle-range hotels. Egyptians need an

ID to stay at a hotel and foreigners must show their passports. A foreigner cannot check in with an Egyptian of the opposite sex without a marriage certificate.

Apartments

Finding an apartment in Cairo is easy. Once settled on the area where you want to live, identify an apartment block you like the look of, and find the *bawwab* (see page 101). He will know about availability of apartments and will be able to introduce you to the landlord. If he warms to you, he can even negotiate for you. Once the lease has been signed, give him a small gratuity. The landlord will also be paying him for finding a tenant. Establish a good relationship with your *bawwab*—you will need him later.

Before agreeing to take an apartment, it is wise to find out if there is a mosque or a school nearby. Mosques broadcast the call to prayer five times a day starting at sunrise. While this can be a beautiful thing, you may not want it coming through a loudspeaker right into your bedroom. Schools sing the national anthem and put out daily digests on a loudspeaker. People do get used to it, and you know you have reached local status once you manage to sleep through the morning sounds. If you are a light sleeper, though, this is something to be aware of.

Most apartments will be furnished. If you don't like the furniture, focus on whether the place is clean, and has good appliances and a working telephone. The landlord can store the furniture.

When the contract for a lease is signed, don't be surprised if the rent stated in the paperwork is lower than the rent you have agreed to pay. It will help the landlord avoid tax and doesn't affect you. Just agree: it will score you points and help to establish a relationship of trust.

HEALTH

There are a few ways to minimize sickness during your stay in Egypt. Don't drink tap water: drink bottled water. Ask for drinks without ice cubes. Avoid undercooked meat on street stalls, and meat from unknown eating establishments. Salad needs to be very well washed in clean water. If buying sandwiches on the street, ask for them to be without salad.

Foreigners should avoid taking a dip in the Nile. The river is a habitat for the parasite that causes the chronic disease bilharziasis, also known as schistosomiasis. Symptoms include muscle pains, diarrhea, fever, vomiting, coughing, and blood in the urine. It is treatable with medication.

Egyptian doctors are well trained, but hygiene in many hospitals is questionable and nurses are inexpert. In nonemergency situations, private clinics are the best option. Most of the time these operate on a first-come first-served basis and doctors are likely to speak English. With better-known consultants, an appointment is required.

SAFETY

Terrorism

Tourism, Egypt's main source of hard currency, has been affected by terrorist attacks since the 1990s. Protective of its tourist industry, the government has taken strict measures to minimize the threat. Metal detectors have been installed at the entries to all tourist sites and hotels. Police are present at all spots frequented by foreigners and undercover police are always present as an extra precaution.

Crime

By Western standards, Egypt is a very safe country. Random violence is rare and visitors often describe how safe they feel walking around, day or night. Pickpocketing and petty crime are on the increase, however, particularly as the economic situation worsens for many. Sensible precautions should be taken.

Women

Foreign women are often misunderstood in this conservative society. Friendly conduct can be interpreted as flirtation, and women out at night without a male escort can give the impression that they are inviting attention. For these reasons foreign women may be harassed on the streets. Most Egyptian women do not show legs, bare arms, or cleavage when out on the street, and you are advised to follow their example. If you are going to a Western-style establishment where it is acceptable to wear revealing clothes, wear a large shawl or a coat on the journey there and back. Abiding by these rules can help minimize, but not always eliminate, harassment.

Most harassment takes the form of whistling, leering, and even groping. Some guidebooks advise women to turn round and shout at the aggressor in Arabic. This is unwise. It will not shame them into stopping but will in fact provoke laughter and possibly more harassment. A woman should not interact with the aggressor. She can either shout out loudly, which will draw enough attention to scare the offender away, or walk away from the situation. Interacting with the harasser one-on-one is unfortunately a no-win situation for a foreign woman. Harassment rarely takes place at tourist resorts and beaches, where people are used to mingling with foreigners.

chapter eight

BUSINESS BRIEFING

Foreign businesspeople are often surprised by the coexistence of modern technology and antiquated business practices in Egypt. Older establishments, with their bureaucracy and officialdom, exist alongside an increasing number of modern businesses and multinational companies.

Sadat's Open Door Policy started the move toward a free market economy. In 2004, the cabinet took major steps to streamline and liberalize the economy, including faster paced privatization, customs reforms, liberalization of the banking industry, and active encouragement of private enterprise. Liberalization is still ongoing and the law is being amended continuously. It is essential to seek professional advice to keep up with the latest rules and regulations. Government Web sites also provide up-to-date information.

The big cities have excellent business facilities. Business centers and rooms at major hotels are equipped with satellite television, fax, printing facilities, and wireless Internet connections.

The pace of business, however, is generally much slower in Egypt than it is in the West. Traditional management style is top–down, with the head of a company acting as decision maker. Trust is vital to any business activity and it takes time to create networks and establish personal relationships.

Private businesses tend to have a five-day workweek, from Sunday to Thursday, but a great many firms work on Saturday. Business hours are from 9:00 a.m. to 5:00 p.m., although smaller businesses start later and may be open until 7:00 or 8.00 p.m. The government sector works six days a week, from Saturday to Thursday,  generally from 8:00 a.m. to 2:00 p.m. All businesses are closed on Friday, the Muslim holy day. Trade unions are closely controlled by the government.

THE BUSINESS LANDSCAPE

The Egyptian business landscape is varied and changing rapidly. Government-owned institutions still exist. The number of family businesses is decreasing, as children and siblings choose to break away from the hereditary structure and move to personally chosen fields. Multinational companies are on the increase, as legislation has made the environment more favorable for investment. There are also many small and medium-sized companies.

Despite the reforms aimed at cutting red tape, Egypt still suffers from practices inherited from the bureaucratic past. Every transaction faces the inevitable obstacles of regulations and delays.

Foreigners wishing to pursue business in Egypt can establish a presence in three ways. They can set up a Limited Liability Company; a Limited Shares Company; or a Joint Stock Company. Alternatively, a representation or branch office can be set up. A local partner, while not required by law, can help penetrate the market, cut through red tape, and untangle the web of bribes and sweeteners. The law requires that an Egyptian agent be used when submitting a tender to a public sector company, but not when dealing with the Ministry of Defense.

BUSINESS CULTURE

Business success depends greatly on the personal dimension. Connections are key. Good personal relationships and trust are needed not only to initiate new ventures, but to ensure the smooth running of existing arrangements. Pleasant rapport paves the way for payments being made on time, for appointments being honored, and for mistakes being corrected swiftly.

Developing business networks is regarded as an essential part of business. Socializing can take place during working hours and in the workweek.

In Egypt, things take time. This is a factor that has frustrated many a foreign visitor. Major decisions are made at the highest level, with the subordinates in charge of initiating business and following up with logistics. Egyptians do not naturally delegate. The more junior the contact, the longer it takes for things to happen, as each employee waits for the green light from his senior. Bureaucracy also slows things down, particularly when dealing with the government.

Understanding the Egyptian rhythm, and working with it rather than against it, can make the difference between success and failure. When problems arise, the maintenance of harmony is the only way to solve them. Foot stamping and issuing ultimatums will not only have a negative effect: it may end the deal altogether. Egyptians will put their pride before their interest. If they feel insulted or patronized, they would rather take their business elsewhere.

When making a complaint, it is important to direct it to the correct level, usually the highest one. Addressing major complaints to subordinates will fall on deaf ears.

Knowledge of English is not automatic among Egyptian businesspeople. Often, the heads of large companies will belong to the more affluent Westernized classes and will speak English. This is not necessarily the case with middle management and government officials, so it is wise to find a translator if you do not already have a local agent.

"SWEETENERS"

High-level corruption is openly discussed in the Egyptian media, and fighting it is a declared government policy. Following corruption scandals several prominent businessmen and public officials are now behind bars.

Low-level corruption, however, is endemic. "Sweeteners" in their many forms are often the price to pay for business. It is a notion that has become deeply woven into the fabric of Egyptian society. Bribery and corruption are common in small- and medium-sized businesses and when dealing with the public sector and government ministries. In the private sector bribery is rare, although invoices can be overstated, with the unspoken consent of the other party. That said, there are many employees or officials who would be insulted to be offered a bribe.

While large businesses and multinational companies have strict codes of conduct and ethics, they are sometimes obliged to abide by the unspoken business rules, turn a blind eye to low-level bribes, or engage in excessive gift giving.

Generally, in order to get something done, a string of licenses, clearances, and permits needs to be obtained. Some form of bribery is expected at many of these bureaucratic junctions. At this level and in the short-term, everyone involved seems to benefit from the practice. The excuse made is that they are helping underpaid functionaries with extra cash in return for speeding up paperwork. And, on their part, the functionaries feel that the privileged business elite can afford to part with their cash, so why not? Many depend on bribes to supplement inadequate salaries; for others it has simply become part of the culture.

"EGYPTIAN STANDARD TIME"

Most appointments run late in Egypt, and people tend to be unpunctual. There are several genuine reasons for this. The major one is traffic congestion, which is highly unpredictable. Rush hours, of course, play a part, but road accidents—which are very common—can create bottlenecks that take hours to unblock. Dignitaries and senior government officials traveling by car also cause immense traffic backlogs, as streets are usually sealed off when they are traveling on the road.

Foreigners are known and expected to be more punctual, and Egyptians will make special efforts to be on time when meeting them. Visitors should try to show up on time but should also expect their contact to be late. If you are running behind, a phone call to notify the contact is polite. To be realistic, one should limit the number of fixed appointments to one or two a day.

BUSINESS ETIQUETTE

Respect

Status and seniority are especially evident in the business environment. Most communications will be formal at first. Addressing someone by their correct title honors that formality and shows respect. It is crucial to find out the correct title of a contact prior to a meeting. A minister, for example, has to be addressed by the title "Your Excellency." Anyone with a doctorate expects to be called "Doctor." Failure to observe these niceties comes across as arrogant, a trait that Egyptians dislike intensely.

Most Egyptians should be addressed by their title and their given name: a Mohammed Hanafi should be addressed *Ustaz* Mohammed or *Ductor* Mohammed. Some, particularly in the services and tourist industries, also use the English Mr., so

Mister Mohammed is also acceptable. In writing, use the title and the full name: *Ustaz Mohammed Hanafi.* It is useful to find out before the meeting how to write your contact's name in English, to facilitate pronunciation.

Business Dress

When it comes to business dress, visitors are expected to observe Egyptian standards of modesty. Men should wear suits and ties to formal or first meetings. Shirts and trousers are acceptable at informal meetings. Jeans and T-shirts are never acceptable. Men with long hair, piercings, or any visible jewelry—other than a wedding ring—are considered unprofessional.

Women should dress conservatively in a business context. It is essential to avoid body-hugging outfits or low necklines. Skirts should be long: make sure they are below the knee when sitting down. Trouser suits are the safest option.

Business Cards

Business cards are the must-have accessory, and are exchanged on every possible occasion. They can be printed quickly and cheaply in Egypt, and it is considered a nice touch to have them printed in both English and Arabic.

Business Gifts

Business gifts are usually exchanged at the end of the year. They are offered to contacts with whom you have developed a professional relationship or wish to do so. Appropriate gifts include elegant stationery or crafts from your own country. Do not be extravagant as this pressures your contact into returning a gift of the same value.

PRESENTATIONS

In Egypt meetings are more usual than presentations because Egyptians prefer talking to listening. But presentations are becoming more common as new technologies and products are being introduced into the country.

When they do take place, they are taken very seriously. In the private sector, the atmosphere is comparable to the Western-style presentation, where disruptions are unlikely and time constraints apply.

When dealing with the government and traditional family businesses, however, older patterns still apply, and you are likely to be interrupted frequently by phone calls, doors opening and closing, and people bringing in papers for signature. Be patient. This does not indicate that your business is unimportant, but in this culture people juggle many things at once.

Although it depends on the situation, it is rare for the top decision maker to be in attendance at presentations, though this may also be affected by the amount of business you are bringing. Generally, it is middle management or heads of department who will be present. Spend five or ten minutes making introductions and conversation. Once the presentation begins, personal anecdotes and stories are not advisable, nor are jokes. Egyptians do not always relate to Western humor but, if a foreigner makes a joke, they will be forced to laugh to avoid embarrassing them. Joking in a presentation setting creates awkwardness.

If the company chief is present, the formality factor increases and the presentation will be short. Get straight to the point. If the top person receives a phone call, stop the presentation and carry on again when he is ready.

The time you have for presentations depends very much on whom you are meeting: the more senior the person the less time you have. Generally presentations can run anywhere between fifteen minutes and an hour. It is wise to ask beforehand how much time you have in order to prepare appropriately.

NEGOTIATIONS

It is important to be aware of two things when negotiating. First, the Arabic language and style is very flowery and expressive. Language will be peppered with hyperbole. "Definitely" can mean "maybe." "Immediately" can mean "soon." It is sometimes wise not to take things too literally.

Second, many people will oversell at first, with the expectation that they will be knocked back. An Egyptian negotiator will be ready to reduce a price at the first sign of hesitation by the visitor. A visitor, on his part, should be prepared to inflate his proposals and be ready to bring them down. This shows a willingness to be flexible—a quality appreciated by Egyptians. When leaving the negotiating table, you should not consider that negotiation is necessarily over. It is up to you to stay in touch regularly.

The negotiations will usually be conducted by middle management. They will communicate the results to senior management, who will close the deal and sign.

CONTRACTS

The Egyptian Civil Code is the prime source of civil law in Egypt. It is derived largely from the French Napoleonic Code. While commercial provisions are included in the law, contracts should be comprehensive and set out all the details. The format will usually be dictated by the stronger party. Contracts will generally be in Arabic, except in rare cases with multinational companies where they will be drafted in English. For court proceedings, English contracts should be translated into Arabic and notarized.

In Egypt, as in the West, contracts are binding and disputes are settled in court. Court proceedings are lengthy and time-consuming, however, so it is recommended that provision for arbitration is included in any agreement. An Egyptian court will respect an arbitration clause. Arbitration may be conducted under any of the internationally recognized sets of rules.

MEETINGS

When arranging a meeting, it is best to book appointments ahead and confirm them closer to the dates. First meetings will be very formal affairs, generally in a place of business. Formal dress and formal forms of address are required. Address your contacts by title and first name until they suggest otherwise.

Meetings are more personal occasions than presentations, so it is considered rude to walk in and get straight down to business. Even first meetings begin with tea or coffee and some conversation on topics such as culture, history, and sports. Avoid subjects like religion, politics, and the Arab–Israeli conflict. If a relationship has already been developed with the contact, it is appropriate to ask about health and family. When referring to family, however, speak generally; do not ask about a wife or a daughter specifically.

Again, unlike presentations, meetings involve animated dialogue that can seem to dip in and out of the subject quite aimlessly. Rarely will there be bullet point discussions. Expect meetings to be patchy, with many disruptions, tea, and more tea. Remain focused, ignore the distractions, and be patient. Egyptians love talking, and use business

meetings to try to impress, often by trumpeting personal achievements. Don't worry; this is only a way of getting down to business, and don't look at your watch, as this is considered rude. Use this time to get to know your contact. Ask questions, but stay away from personal topics.

After the first meeting, it is very important to follow up with phone calls, both to make sure that the business is being carried forward and to have a personal talk with the other party.

After several communications, your contact may suggest moving the meeting from the office to a café or less formal setting. This means that you have moved up the confidence ladder and the relationship is taking on a more informal nature.

Never leave a meeting on a business note: make another few minutes of social talk.

Time Is Not Money

A foreign executive came to Egypt on private business. He hired an Egyptian advisor to assist him, who arranged a meeting with an Egyptian businessman at the latter's home. Everyone sat down in the formal seating area.

The Egyptian wanted to talk generally and get to know the foreigner before addressing matters of substance. He offered tea and an array of cakes and pastries, and the best china was brought out for the foreign visitor. The foreigner, not wishing to waste his host's time, declined to eat and tried to push on with the subject of his business.

At the end of the meeting the foreigner left frustrated because little had been discussed, and the Egyptian felt that his hospitality had been snubbed. The Egyptian called the advisor and asked that he not arrange any more meetings with the foreigner.

DEALING WITH THE GOVERNMENT

The government exercises a great deal of control over the business environment. It appoints boards of directors of public sector corporations, or companies that are partly state owned. Sometimes, it will not put a tender out to public bidding but will appoint a particular company to take the job. Chairmen of privately owned companies network closely with ministers.

When negotiating with the government, remember that things can be vetoed from the top. There is little transparency in government institutions so one can be subject to arbitrary decisions at any stage before signing a contract.

WOMEN IN BUSINESS

Women in managerial positions still struggle to be accepted and taken seriously. While the law does not discriminate against women in work, society puts pressure on them to be a homemaker first and a professional second. The number of women in senior positions is increasing, but it is rare to find a woman with the final decision-making power in a large company.

Egyptian women expect to be treated as professional equals. However, guidelines for dealing with businesswomen differ dramatically from those with businessmen. Avoid any sign of intimacy. Inviting a female contact out for dinner is a step beyond the business context.

SOCIALIZING

Egyptians are hospitable and will look after their foreign visitors. You will generally not be invited into a contact's home, as the domestic sphere is reserved for close friends and family. It is rare for spouses to attend business lunches and dinners.

No matter how Westernized the social setting, remember that this is a conservative society. Some businesmen may drink. But if you don't know that is the case, it is essential to wait for your contact to be the one to suggest alcohol.

Lunches and dinners start late in Egypt. Lunch can be served as late as 5:00 p.m. and dinner can be served at 10:00 p.m. To socialize over meals, one should be prepared to spend a lot of time outside the office. Generally, whoever has extended the invitation should pay the bill.

chapter nine

COMMUNICATING

LANGUAGE

Arabic is Egypt's official language. It is spoken throughout the Arab world and studied throughout the Islamic world as it is the language of the Qur'an. Arab countries have two forms of Arabic: literary Arabic, used in the media, books, and taught at schools; and the country's own colloquial dialect. The dialects can differ so much from country to country that an Algerian may have trouble understanding an Egyptian; to solve this problem they resort to literary Arabic.

In Egypt, daily life is conducted in colloquial Egyptian, used by shops, taxis, restaurants, and businesses. But formal correspondence is in literary Arabic, also referred to as Modern Standard Arabic.

Many language courses offer foreigners both Modern Standard Arabic and colloquial Egyptian. Some even do tailor-made packages that include both. Listings in Egypt's English-language magazines usually include language classes and

Arabic tutors. Embassies also have information on good Arabic tutors.

In the areas frequented by tourists, many people will speak basic English, and some foreigners find themselves able to get by in Egypt without a single word of Arabic. But Egyptians warmly appreciate the efforts of those who try to speak their language. Making mistakes is fine: it is actually found quite charming and people will extend more courtesy to those who have made the effort to learn some Arabic, even a few words.

The Westernized upper classes will generally speak English, and many will speak French as well. In fact, eavesdrop at any upmarket café and watch as the customers dip in and out of different languages in a single sentence, communicating in some sort of Arabic-English Esperanto.

MANNERS

In Egypt, attitude overrides vocabulary. The Egyptians are a polite people, and good manners envelop their every interaction. True engagement with Egyptian society is possible for a foreigner who has understood and reciprocates these courtesies. Respect is at the heart of good manners. Addressing people by their correct title and showing deference to seniority in position and age is the norm.

Egyptians are helpful by nature. If asked for something, they must oblige. And sometimes they will do so even when not asked. For example, ask for directions in the street and, before you know it, a crowd has gathered and is engaged in earnest debate about the best possible route for you.

Egyptian men will not necessarily open a door or pull out a chair for a woman. The Egyptian idea of gallantry is one of protection. A foreign woman should not be offended if her Egyptian male companion walks in front of her in the street rather than next to her, because he is actually trying to shield her from the crowds. An Egyptian man will never let a woman walk to her car alone after an evening out, and will certainly not let her take a cab home unaccompanied.

Always Offer!

A young Middle Eastern man caught a taxi in downtown Cairo. He was eating a chocolate bar when he climbed in. After a few minutes, the cab driver said to him, "You know how I know you are not Egyptian? If you were you would have offered me some of your chocolate." The young man explained that the chocolate bar was half-eaten and he didn't want to offend the cab driver by offering him it. "An Egyptian would have offered it anyway," said the cab driver.

Egyptians love smoking, which is generally allowed, even in such unlikely places as hospitals and on public transportation. An Egyptian smoker will always offer cigarettes to others. In fact, they will always offer whatever they have to those present. Women, however, are disapproved of if they smoke in public, particularly by the older generation, except in the fashionable cafés and bars of the larger cities.

Egyptians behave conservatively in public. Displays of affection between members of the opposite sex, as we have seen, are taboo. It is mainly the honor of the woman that is at stake. Women who exhibit their emotions in public spaces are seen as loose. At the same time, it is common to see two men hugging and kissing in the street or walking down the street holding hands (with no suggestion of a sexual relationship).

Egyptians generally speak loudly. This is a sign of strength, while speaking softly indicates hesitation. People make eye contact when talking—it shows interest and trust. Someone who doesn't make eye contact is considered untrustworthy. But assertiveness is limited to the volume of speech. Other forms of behavior, considered positive in the West, like being direct and forward, are seen as aggressive and rude. Diplomacy is key to effective communication.

In conversation, good posture is important. Slouching shows a lack of respect. Putting your feet up or crossing your legs in a way that exposes the soles of your shoes is incredibly rude, especially in front of seniors. When in a group setting, presenting your back to someone is rude. And if you have to do so for whatever reason, you should apologize to the person you are doing it to.

The sense of personal space in Egypt differs from that in the West. People tend to sit closer to each other and may be more tactile, but not with the opposite sex. Don't back away—this would imply that you find your counterpart offensive, and would make you appear cold. Warmth is important. Hand gestures are common, and are often used to highlight a point.

SERVICES
Telephone
Communication in Egypt has improved vastly since the 1980s. The installation of modern and efficient telephone systems now make calling just about anywhere in the world as easy as in the West. For directory inquiries, dial 140 from any land line or cell phone.

Emergency Phone Numbers

These are not often used, and operators answering calls speak Arabic only.

Police 122

Ambulance 123

Fire 125

Tourist Police 126

Cell phone networks in Egypt work on GSM and cover most of the country. Handset sales have surged in the last few years. There are currently two cell phone networks in the country, Mobinil and Vodaphone, with preparations for a third under way. Prepaid cards are available at many shops and kiosks. Getting a postpaid line requires some paperwork but can be done.

Pay phones are not very common, though private companies are now increasing this service. You can also make phone calls to a local landline or a cell phone from shops and cigarette kiosks. They charge by the minute.

Mail

The postal system is relatively efficient for international mail. Airmail takes about five days to Western Europe, and about ten days to the U.S.A. But a small percentage of letters or packages don't arrive, so when sending something important it is best to use registered mail at the local post office. Packages are often opened at customs. Books will often be checked for illegal material and CDs are treated suspiciously. Sometimes items in packages might go astray; this depends very much on their resale value.

It's best to send letters from a major city or hotel; blue mailboxes are for overseas airmail, red ones for domestic post. Stamps can be purchased at post offices or hotels. Private courier firms such as Federal Express or DHL are limited to a few cities, and a lot more expensive.

To have mail sent to you, it should bear your name, apartment or house number, street, followed by area, then city, and finally country.

Internet

There is currently an Internet boom in Egypt. Internet access is available in almost all the main tourist destinations, with Internet cafés on the increase everywhere, including in rural areas.

In homes, anyone with a phone line and a modem can connect to the Internet either by subscribing to an Internet Service Provider or by using one of the many free numbers. Many Internet cafés have high-speed connections and the more expensive free wireless: anyone whose computer is Wi-Fi enabled can connect free at any of these cafés. Usually there will be a sign if the café has Wi-Fi.

THE MEDIA

Egypt has long enjoyed the reputation of the cultural capital of the Arab world. It is home to the largest publishing houses in the region. Egypt's oldest newspaper, *Al Ahram*, together with *Al Akhbar* and *Al Gomhouria*, are the three main government-owned newspapers and those with the largest circulations. A number of independent papers also exist, a popular newcomer on the scene being the liberal *Al Masry el Youm*. Many weekly and monthly newspapers and magazines are published in Egypt and are widely available at newsstands and bookshops. All newspapers and magazines are subject to review by the government's Supreme Press Council.

The arrival of Arabic satellite television broadcasters like al-Jazeera and al-Arabiya and the recent mood of reform has meant that censorship rules have relaxed a little, but there is still no criticism of the president, of the military, or anything that can harm national unity. Egypt's emergency law and laws on libel can result in prison sentences for journalists. This means that many exercise a degree of self-censorship.

CONCLUSION

Egyptian people are warm, friendly, funny, and relaxed. On the surface, the way of life of the professional classes is not wildly different from the West, but we have seen something of the subtleties and complexities of their culture.

On a daily basis, most Egyptians endure difficult conditions and remain resilient, taking knocks and springing back up with a determined optimism and good nature. Theirs is a huge untapped potential, waiting to be unleashed. Egypt could achieve greatness again if a solution could be found to its grinding poverty.

For Westerners, flexibility, when it comes to appointments and commitments, is necessary. The Egyptians' apparent passivity and fatalistic attitude, which can sometimes leave foreigners frustrated, is more than balanced by their good humor and positive outlook. They value good relationships, they are loyal to their friends, and welcoming to their visitors. As they say, "Anyone who drinks from the water of the Nile is sure to come back."

Further Reading

Al-Sayyid Marsot, Afaf Lutfi. *A Short History of Modern Egypt.* Cambridge: Cambridge University Press, 1985.

Durrell, Lawrence. *The Alexandria Quartet.* London: Faber and Faber, 1962.

Ghali, Waguih. *Beer in the Snooker Club.* London: Andre Deutsch, 1964.

Heikal, Mohamed H. *Cutting the Lion's Tail: Suez through Egyptian Eyes.* Arbour House Publishing Co, 1987.

Hourani, Albert. *A History of the Arab Peoples.* London: Faber and Faber, 1991.

Idris, Yusuf. *City of Love and Ashes.* Cairo: The American University in Cairo Press, 1998.

Lane, Edward William. *An Account of the Manners and Customs of the Modern Egyptians.* London, 1836.

Mahfouz, Naguib. *The Cairo Trilogy.* Cairo: The American University in Cairo Press, 2001.

Rodenbeck, Max. *Cairo the City Victorious.* London: Picador, 1998.

Soueif, Ahdaf. *In the Eye of the Sun.* London: Bloomsbury, 1992.

Complete Arabic: The Basics. New York: Living Language, 2005.

In-Flight Arabic. NewYork: Living Language, 2001.

Index

Acknowledgements

For Ihab, with all my love.
Thank you for all the help in writing this book.

The Customer Service Companion

This book is
the personal property of:

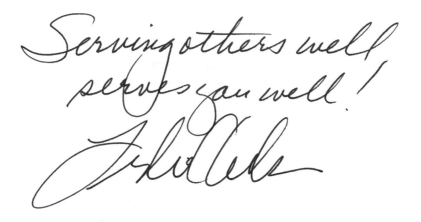

Serving others well,
serves you well!

Also by C. Leslie Charles

STICK TO IT!
The Power of Positive Persistence
ISBN 9644621-0-9

The
**CUSTOMER SERVICE
COMPANION
Study Guide**
ISBN 9644621-2-5

Minspirations
A collection of twelve
inspirational mini-posters
suitable for framing